AF208051

Especially for Charles Moss,
a tale about longhorns, cowboys,
Indians, buffalo hunters & outlaws!!.
Pleasant reading and God bless you,

Derald Mc.Cathern
11-19-99

Dry Bones

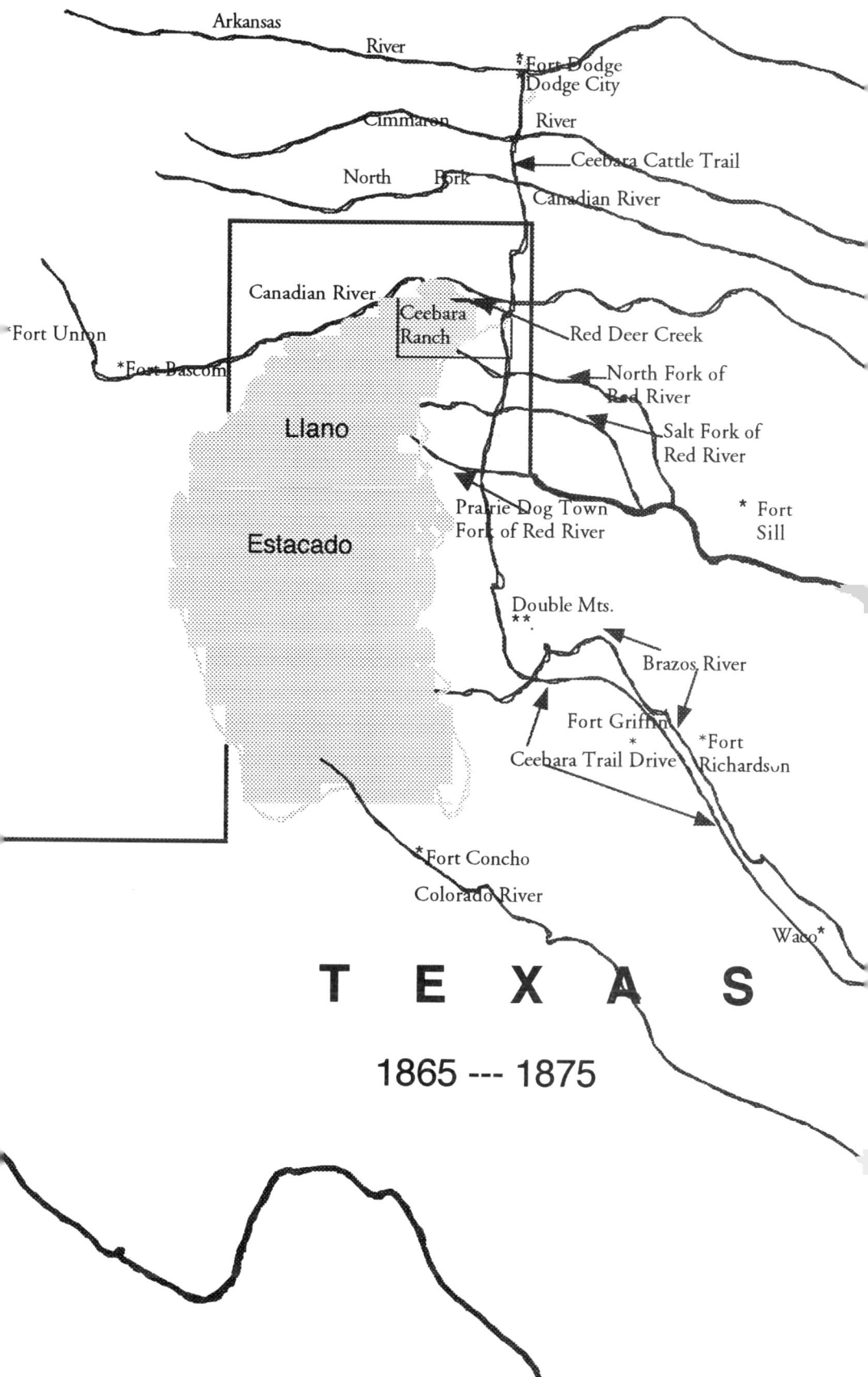

Dry Bones

a Novel by

Gerald McCathern

Copyright 1999 by Gerald McCathern
First Printing 1999

ISBN 0-9656946-2-3
Library of Congress Cat. No. 99-093392

Published by
Outlaw Books
419 Centre Street
Hereford, Tx 79045

Phone 806-364-2838
FAX 806-364-5522
outlawbooks.net
gmccath@wtrt.net

Other Books by Gerald McCathern

Horns
A western historical novel circa 1865-1875
Hardcover

Quarantine
A story of murder and terrorism in the
cattle feeding industry.

From the White House to the Hoosegow
Personal account of the great farmer
protest movement of 1977-1978
Paperback

Gentle Rebels
Farmer's protest and great tractorcade
to Washington, D.C. 1977-1979
Hardcover

To Kill the Goose
Is the U.S heading for food shortages?
Why and how to prevent it.
Hardcover

Order from
Gerald McCathern
419 Centre Street
Hereford, Tx 79045
pho. 806-364-2838

For Charles Moss enjoy the adventure Justin Wells

COVER ART
by Justin Wells

Justin Wells of Amarillo, Texas, likes to do one thing-- draw horses. More specifically, he draws the people, animals and landscapes associated with the horse culture of the American West.

Justin has exhibited his work in galleries and museums in Texas, Oklahoma, New Mexico, Colorado, Wyoming, California and Arizona, and he has contributed illustrations for Western history magazines including *The Westerner* and *The Western Horseman*. A wood-cut titled *Chuckwagon* was featured in John Meig's *The Cowboy in American Prints*.

Original and limited edition reproductions may be obtained by writing Justin Wells Studio, 2712 East 3rd Street, Amarillo, TX 79104 or call 806-373-0889

"The Hoodlum Wagon." Justin Wells.

Acknowledgements

Thanks to all those writers of history who have preserved the events and the lives of the people of the old west for our education and enjoyment--especially writers such as J. Evetts Haley (*Charles Goodnight, Cowman and Plainsman*), C.L. Douglas (*Cattle Kings of Texas*), J. Frank Dobie (*The Longhorns*), Pauline Durrett Robertson and R.L. Robertson (*Panhandle Pilgrimage*), and Fredric R. Young, (*Dodge City*).

I highly recommend these books to readers who are interested in western history.

I also wish to thank the Panhandle Plains Historical Museum in Canyon, Texas, whose archives are full of authenticated historical documents of the old west, which were invaluable in telling the story of *Dry Bones*.

A special thanks to my editor, Virginia Lee, for smoothing the rough spots of *Dry Bones*, and to Cathleen Baldauf for her excellent work in designing the cover.

And a special thanks to all of my reader friends who urged me to continue the story of Cole and Armstrong, their fictional ranch, Ceebara, and their association with the great Comanche Chief, Quanah Parker.

Gerald McCathern
Hereford, Texas
June 29, 1999

Dedicated to my children and grandchildren, who I love dearly.
Mike, and his son and daughter Michael and Amber.
Kathy, her husband Larry Parker, and their children Tara, Trae, and Tyler.
Kolleen, her husband Scott Newland, and their children, Sydnea, Brodie, and Kian.

And to my dear wife, Bonnie, who has, for 52 years, been the light of my life.

About *Dry Bones*

Dry Bones is a work of fiction based on actual historical events which occurred in Texas, Oklahoma, Kansas and New Mexico, during the years 1875-1881. Most of the action takes place in and around the wild and lawless towns of Mobeetie, Tascosa, and Dodge City.

Although I have tried to keep historical events as accurate as possible, while spinning an exciting fictional tale about the old west, you may find some of the dates out of place. However, recorded history does place them all within the six year time frame of 1875-1881.

There are many historical characters in *Dry Bones*, although information about their activities in the Texas Panhandle were sometimes mere speculation on the part of historical writers. For instance, it is well documented that William Bonney (Billy the Kid) spent time in Tascosa and Mobeetie--and that he stole horses and rustled cattle, but the particulars of those episodes are sketchy, at best.

Heinrich Borne (Dutch Henry), buffalo hunter, who fought with Bat Masterson and Billy Dixon at the Battle of Adobe Walls, is known to have taken the outlaw trail; robbing, stealing horses and cattle, and killing those who took offense at his shenanigans. However, little is known about where and when he pursued his illegal activities.

Quanah Parker, the half white notorious Comanche Chief, is known to have made many trips back to the *Llano Estacado* after the Indians had been banished to the reservations in Oklahoma Territory. Because the Indians had no written language, much speculation has been drawn about his activities during those forays.

And so I apologize, dear reader, if events are somewhat embellished in *Dry Bones*. I agree with a statement I once heard Elmer Kelton make:

"If it didn't happen this way, it should have."

--IT HAS BEEN SAID--

"OTHER STATES WERE CARVED OR BORN,
TEXAS GREW FROM HIDE AND HORN"

Berta Hart Nance

Foreword

The eagle soared lazily, riding the updrafts along the edge of the caprock, looking for food in the form of an unwary jack rabbit or perhaps a fat field mouse. He could feed on one of the many thousands of rotting buffalo carcasses which dotted the flat plains for as far as his eyes could see, but he preferred the warm flesh of a small live animal. He would just as soon leave the buffalo carcasses to the buzzards and the coyotes.

He could remember, just ten summers before, when there were no dead buffalo scarring his hunting grounds. That was before the white man had invaded the plains and began slaughtering the millions of head of migrating shaggies which annually moved across the huge grasslands known as the *Llano Estacado*. He remembered that was during a time of peace, a time when his friends, the noble red men, hunted the buffalo for food, clothing and shelter. They killed only what they needed, saving the hide for their clothing and lodges, the meat to fill their bellies when they were hungry, the entrails for thread and utensils and the bones for tools and weapons. When the Indians left a kill area, there was little left on the prairie to indicate that another buffalo had been killed.

The white men came and, with their big guns, began

slaughtering the herds, taking only the hides and the tongues and leaving the rest to rot. Now, on this warm spring day in 1875, the buffalo were destined for extinction, with thousands of white hunters trailing and slaughtering the last of the herds. From his lofty position high above the prairie, he could see only a few thousand of the black animals grazing where there had been millions, and he could also see the wagons of the white men trailing the small herds, now and again hear the roar of the huge buffalo guns and see more of his friends, the buffalo, fall dead--victims of the lead of the huge guns.

Off to the right and just below the caprock, the eagle could see the first signs of permanent settlement in his land by the white man. Army tents and sod and picket houses were being erected along the headwaters of the Sweetwater Creek. His friends, the red men, after ten years of war, had finally been defeated by the horse soldiers, driven back east into the land called Indian Territory, and the soldiers had built a fort along the creek for the purpose of protecting the white hunters and to be certain that the Indians did not return to the *Llano Estacado*, their sacred hunting grounds.

A large cotton wood tree on the banks of the creek had been the eagle's perch as he rested on his hunting forays for many years and he had noticed on the trunk of the tree a deep scar cut into the bark by one of the first white men to come into the area. As he slowly descended, wings outstretched to hold his huge body, he once again settled graciously onto the topmost branch of the tree, noticing that the strange looking scar was still present and had grown with time as the tree had grown.

Neither the eagle nor the red men could understand its meaning, but other white men could -- C __ A, C - Bar - A, the same letters he could see burned on the hips of the thousands of longhorn cattle which now dotted the plains.

Within hours after the erection of the fort, named Fort Elliot, a small community outside the fort's perimeter, began to take form. The first business erected was merely a huge tent with a makeshift sign proclaiming it to be a saloon and advertising its wares as *whiskey and women*. The eagle, interested in this new addition to his land, watched as dirty and filthy buffalo hunters rushed across the prairie to be the first customers of this new establishment. Their camp, where they had brought their wagons loaded with buffalo hides to sell to teamsters who hauled them to the rail head in Dodge City, was located just across the Sweetwater Creek from the fort, surrounding the huge cottonwood tree where he was perched. The fly-infested camp was known as Hide Town.

To the north the eagle could see a long string of wagons heading for the fort, carrying supplies from Dodge City. Later, the wagons would return to Dodge City loaded with the dried hides of the slaughtered buffalo, and the hunters would have their pockets full of gold coins to spend on the whiskey and painted ladies in the newly erected saloon.

Although the eagle paid little heed, already the semblance of a town was beginning to form to replace the buffalo hunters' camp. The town site was to be named Mobeetie, an Indian word meaning *Sweetwater*. But the sweet water which flowed inside the city limits of Mobeetie for several years to come would be whiskey, for most of the new establishments would be saloons -- eventually to number thirteen. Not only would the soldiers and hunters be well supplied with strong liquor, the saloon-keepers would bring in over five hundred lovely young *ladies of the night* who would lure them into their bedrooms and relieve them of additional gold coins in return for sharing their beds and a night of pleasure.

The eagle remembered well the first Anglo people to come into his domain ten years before, two cattlemen who would establish the first cattle ranch twenty-five miles north of the location of the new fort, on Red Deer Creek. But these Anglos did not bring death and desolation to the area. They made friends with the ruling Indian tribe, the Comanches, and promised chief Quanah Parker that they would live peacefully with him and his tribe, respecting their land and their buffalo.

The two cowboys, ex-confederate colonel Jim Cole and his young side-kick, Ned Armstrong, gained permission from the Indians to build their ranch and to bring up five thousand head of longhorn cattle from Central Texas, promising Quanah that any time the buffalo were not present in the area, the tribe could use whatever beef they needed for food.

The ranch, Ceebara, so named for the C-Bar-A brand, prospered and offspring of the herd were driven each year to the railhead at Dodge City for shipment to markets back east. The Indians were satisfied and the cattlemen were satisfied but that all ended when the U.S. Army encouraged the buffalo hunters to invade the area and begin slaughtering the huge buffalo herds. Quanah organized all of the tribes, Comanches, Cheyennes, Kiowas and Apaches, into a formidable army to fight the hunters and the cavalry, and for over five years was able to remain on the plains. But eventually, the overbearing strength of the federal government was too great, the soldiers too many and the guns too large for the Indians to survive.

The eagle watched sadly as his friends were defeated in a final battle in the depths of the Palo Duro Canyon and were forced to flee back to safety inside the newly established reservations in Indian Territory. With no protection from the tribes, the buffalo herds were systematically being destroyed by the hunters and the *Llano Estacado* was opened for settlement.

The eagle would have been disturbed had he known that this was just the beginning of a total change in his land. The buffalo hunters would eventually kill the last of the huge herds of buffalo, leaving their bones to dry and turn white from exposure to the sun and wind, and other cattlemen would begin invading the area, competing with Cole and Armstrong for possession of millions of acres of the huge grasslands. Longhorned cattle would be brought in by the hundreds of thousands to replace the buffalo, and cowboys would replace the Indians and the buffalo hunters.

And like the buffalo, the eagle was destined to be destroyed.

1

The kid rode into Hidetown, a small community on the banks of the Sweetwater Creek in the Texas Panhandle, with a string of eight horses trailing behind. He rode into town warily, looking right and left down the sandy street, as if expecting trouble. Or perhaps, just to be prepared if trouble came. For this was tough country where the dregs of western humanity had chosen to establish a place of commerce. A place where thousands of buffalo hides were brought in daily by hunters, to be stretched and dried and sold to freighters who carried them on wagons to market at Dodge City, one hundred and thirty miles to the north.

Stopping at the hitching rail of the Lady Gay Saloon, he dismounted and tied the horses to the rail. The ride from Atascosa Crossing had been long, hot and dusty and he was ready for a drink to wash the dirt from his throat. He removed his hat, wiped the sweat from his brow, then used the hat to beat some of the dust off his sweat streaked shirt and chaps.

Ned, with Sonny and Miguel, had arrived from Ceebara headquarters only a few minutes before him, and they were loading supplies into the wagon in front of the mercantile, which was located next door to the Lady Gay.

Actually, the mercantile was surrounded by saloons, Hidetown boasting eleven of the establishments, catering to the wishes of the buffalo hunters, the soldiers from nearby Fort Elliot, the teamsters from Dodge City and now, the cowboys from Ceebara--the first cattle ranch established in the unsettled and uncharted Texas Panhandle.

Although in its infancy, Hidetown was like most frontier towns, with an abundance of saloons which were well stocked with whiskey, beer and *painted* ladies--a place where the gold paid for buffalo hides could be exchanged for the wishes of the wild and tough men who plied the trade. The rough hewn tables within the saloons were always crowded with card sharps, hunters and soldiers--betting their money and sometimes their lives on a turn of the cards. And the rooms at the back of the bar were always filled with the *painted* ladies, where they entertained anyone, with a gold coin in his pocket, for a share of their newly found wealth.

Ned Armstrong and Colonel Jim Cole, founders of Ceebara, had met on the battlefield in Virginia at the end of the Civil War, where the Colonel had lost his right arm to canon grape. Ned had nursed him back to health and traveled with him back to Texas, where they laid claim to a million acres of lush grasslands in the Texas Panhandle, land which had been a grant to the Colonel by the legislature of the Republic of Texas, back in 1844. For the past ten years, since 1865, the Colonel and Ned had carved out a working ranch in this frontier area, a stronghold of the Comanche Indians, by making friends with the great Comanche Chief, Quanah Parker.

The Red River Wars between the Indians and white buffalo hunters and the U.S. Army had ended, and the last of the tribes, Quanah Parker's Kwahadi Comanches, had been forced onto the reservations in the Oklahoma Territory. Without the impediment of the ferocious Indians, buffalo hunters accelerated their systematic slaughter of the millions of buffalo roaming the grasslands of the Texas Panhandle.

Hidetown, on the Sweetwater Creek, had sprung up as a gathering place where the hide hunters could deliver their hides to buyers who in turn hauled them over the Ceebara Trail (later to be named the Jones-Plummer Trail) to the railhead at Dodge City.

It was a wide-open frontier town with absolutely no law, a place where the weak and the meek dare not tarry--a place where gun shots could be heard hourly and graves were dug daily. It quickly became known as the roughest and wildest town in the west-- a sin town where nothing was sacred. It did, however, offer the nearest place for the cowboys to buy supplies for the ranch, less than a days ride from ranch headquarters.

Colonel Cole had cautioned his cowboys, and especially Ned, to steer clear of the troublemakers in the town. Before the war with the Yankees, he had been a part of the wild bunch that had fought for Texas' freedom from the Mexicans, having been the youngest member of the band of *Texicans* that holed up in the Alamo. Only by fate, and the need for someone to carry a message out of the mission to General Sam Houston, was he able to escape the massacre that befell his comrades. Colonel Travis and his friend Davy Crockett, had placed him, a green sixteen-year-old kid, on the fastest horse in the Alamo and slipped him out under the cover of darkness. What he and the horse couldn't outrun, they jumped over, and he was able to get through the Mexicans' lines and delivered the message to Houston. Before he could return, the Mexicans overran the mission and the Alamo became history.

His association with Crockett, Bowie, Travis and the rest of that wild bunch taught him to use the six shooter with the best of them, and he had built a reputation of being one of the fastest guns in Texas, before he rode off with a group of Texas volunteers to fight alongside General Lee in the war.

"Steer clear of that bunch of hunters in Hidetown," he had told Ned. "If they try to start something, just turn and walk away. They'd as soon shoot you in the back as look at you. I know I taught you to use your guns for protection, and you're probably as fast and as straight as anyone, but if you tangle with one of those hunters, you're liable to have the whole wolf pack on your back."

Ned looked up from his work as he stacked another sack of beans into the bed of the wagon and watched as the kid tied his string of horses to the rail. They were beautiful horses, tall and muscular and showing the looks of good cow ponies. One gray stallion, especially, caught Ned's eye. He was always looking for good horses to add to Ceebara's remuda -- and especially good stallions to crossbreed to their mares.

Walking over, he spoke, "Howdy -- good looking set of horses. Don't suppose they're for sale?"

The kid smiled and answered, "Maybe, if'n the price is right."

Ned stuck out his hand, "Ned Armstrong from the Ceebara ranch over on Red Deer Creek."

"Bonney, Billy Bonney, but most folks just call me Kid," the stranger answered, smiling as he took Ned's hand, then added, "Heard they was a ranch over in these here parts. I guess those longhorns I passed up on top of the plains carrying that C Bar A brand must be a part of your herd. Sure was a helluva lot of 'em, they was strung out from here clean up to that buffalo hunters camp at Atascosa Crossing on the Canadian."

Ned couldn't help but notice that the kid's Colt was slung low and tied down in the style that gun slingers wore. *Another hot-head looking to get himself killed,* Ned thought. *Especially here in Hidetown, there's a hundred toughs here who would like an opportunity to build their reputation by adding one more notch to their guns by taking on a green kid like this in a showdown.*

"Buy you a drink?" Ned asked, as he walked around the horses, looking each over closely, then added, "We might just see if my dollars fit your horses."

"Best deal I've been offered all day," the kid answered as he led the way through the swinging doors of the Lady Gay. They pushed through the crowd of buffalo hunters and soldiers and walked up to the bar.

"Hello, Jake," Ned greeted the bartender.

"Howdy, Ned, heard you was in town. How's the Colonel these days?"

"Ornery as ever, Jake. Me and Sonny and Miguel thought we'd ride in for supplies and get away from his snarling," Ned joked.

"Well, Jones and Plummer brought in a new load of goods by freight wagon just yesterday. Should be able to get what you need," the bartender said, then added, "What'll it be?"

"Just give us a bottle of your best, we're going to see if we can do some horse swapping."

Ned and the Kid walked to a table in the corner and sat down. Ned had never liked hard liquor and seldom drank, but knew it was sociable to share a drink when horse trading was involved--and he knew this stranger had a strong thirst built up after a long, dry ride across the prairie. He poured two glasses and was surprised when the kid turned his up and downed it in one gulp, pushing the glass forward for a refill.

"I worked up a mighty thirst up there on the plains," he said as he pushed his hat to the back of his head and wiped the sweat from his brow with the back of his hand.

Under the covering of dust which covered his body, Ned could see that the Kid was a rather handsome fellow, had it not been for the protrusion of his two front teeth. Although short in stature, probably no more than five feet six inches tall, the Kid appeared to be very muscular and stout. His dark, unruly hair, stuck from beneath his hat and fell across his brow. His smile was infectious, one that invited friendship. But his eyes--there was something hidden there in their depths that seemed to say, "I'd like to be your friend, but I've learned that friends sometime betray you."

6

"Where you from, Kid," Ned asked as he sipped his drink.

"Around," came the answer.

Ned didn't push, most folks found in towns like Hidetown were not too prone to speak about their past, where they were from or where they were going. If the Kid had secrets he could keep them as far as Ned was concerned. The Kid had horses for sale and he was interested in buying horses.

As they sat at the rough table, each looking squarely into the other's eyes, Ned asked, "What's your price?"

"One or all?" the Kid asked.

"All."

"Guess you noticed that big gray -- helluva horse. I'm gonna have to have a hundred for him, the others fifty apiece."

"That'd be four-fifty for the string?"

"*Si,*" the Kid replied, reverting to a soft, Spanish accent, smiling.

But he's not Mexican, Ned thought, *must be from down along the border or maybe over Santa Fe way.* "Three-fifty would fit my dollars better," he said.

"*No Bueno, Senor,* but maybe we could talk about splitting it. Four hundred."

Pushing his hand across the table, Ned nodded his head in agreement and said, "Deal." *May be just a green kid,* he thought, *but he knows horses and knows how to make a deal.* His respect for the youngster was growing.

Ned failed to notice six tough looking drifters seated at a table across the room who were watching the transaction with too much interest. It was apparent that they, too, were interested in the Kid's horses.

Ned and the Kid walked out of the saloon into the bright sunlight of the West Texas day and strode toward the horses tied to the rail. Deer flies were pestering the horses and they were swishing their tails, and now and then stomping their hooves to keep the flies airborne.

A small whirlwind twisted across the street kicking up a trail of dust as a black cur dog,, caught in the twisting dirt, tucked his tail between his legs and crawled under the wagon. Ned pulled four, one hundred dollar gold coins from the leather pocket of his buckskin chaps and handed them to the young horse trader.

"Guess I'll need a bill of sale," he said as the money changed hands.

The Kid smiled and said, "You write it, I'll sign it."

Ned pulled a pencil and paper from his shirt pocket and wrote, "*Eight horses, one large gray stallion, three sorrel geldings, three bay mares and one blazed face black filly with three stocking feet, sold to Ned Armstrong for four hundred dollars by Billy Bonney, whose signature is signed below. No apparent brands or marks on any of the horses.*"

The Kid signed it and returned the paper to Ned as the six tough looking, dirty drifters stepped from the saloon and walked towards the horses. They stopped about twenty paces away from Ned and the Kid. The leader of the group, a huge bull of a man with long, black, unkempt hair and scraggly beard spoke with a growl, "Them looks like my horses that some horse thief stole from me a week ago up on the Arkansas." The deep, crescent shaped scar across his cheek pulled the corner of his mouth down into a wicked looking snarl as he spoke.

The Kid stepped away from the horses where he could see all six of the men standing with legs spread apart and their hands hanging close to the butts of their Colts which were slung low on their hips.

"You must be mistaken, mister," he said coolly, "I trailed a couple dozen head from New Mexico over to Atascosa and sold all of them to buffalo hunters except these eight head. Them buffalo hunters didn't know a good horse from a bad one and I still got the top end of the herd."

"I ain't mistaken, you're a horse thief and them's my horses," the scar-faced leader replied.

Ned could see that the scar-faced renegade was pushing for a showdown that would draw the Kid into a gunfight in which he would be outnumbered and outgunned.

The five drifters, who backed the speaker, fidgeted nervously as they observed the Kid's coolness.

"Just a minute, mister," Ned interrupted. "I just bought them horses and they don't belong to either one of you, they're mine until you can prove otherwise. I don't see no brand that says they're yours."

Ned was quite a contrast to the dark haired Kid. Six feet tall, a little on the skinny side, with well groomed blonde hair which hung from under his hat, nearly shoulder length.

"I don't have to prove nothing to you, cowboy. Me and my partners say they're mine, and we're taking them now."

The Kid had slowly moved away from Ned, all the while watching the hands of the six drifters. Ned, caught up in the argument, knew that the Kid's eyes were riveted on the big man, so he shifted his eyes to the other five as he slowly moved away from the horses, watching to see if they were going to back up their leader.

Sonny and Miguel, hearing the argument, moved quickly to the side of the street and caught the attention of two of the renegades, who nervously moved their hands away from their guns and hitched their fingers in their gun belts. Sonny smiled, and nodded to the gunmen that he expected them to keep their hands in that position.

The big man's fingers twitched and his eyes blinked nervously. His eyes gave him away as he grabbed for his gun. The Kid's gun was in his hand before the big man's Colt ever broke leather, spewing lead into his adversary's chest.

Ned had been watching the other two gunmen who were standing next to the leader. As they made their move, in a flash his gun was in his hand and firing. Both of the gunmen went down from Ned's quick shots, guns half drawn, their eyes open in death. The Kid's Colt spit lead at another who had his gun out and was firing. Blood stained the Kid's shirt just above the belt and close to the left side. As he was knocked backwards, his shot found its mark in the gunman's throat, sending him spinning to the side. The astonished drifter dropped his gun and grabbed his throat in an effort to stop the flow of blood -- to no avail. His scream was drowned in his own blood as it squirted between his fingers -- with his mouth open unbelieving,, his knees buckled and he fell face forward into the dirt of the street and gasped his last breath. Sonny quickly drew his Colt and turned it towards the other two gunmen who had thrown their empty hands above their heads and were shouting, "Don't shoot, don't shoot. We ain't a part of this fight." Motioning towards the big man lying in a pool of blood, the slim one said, "Those horses don't belong to him, he just thought the kid would be easy pickins and we could take his herd without a fight."

Sonny and Miguel, guns in their hands, relieved the two remaining gunmen of their weapons as Ned turned to help the Kid who was now kneeling and holding his hand over the flesh wound, trying to stop the bleeding.

"O.K., you two hombres pick up your dead friends and find some place to plant 'em, then mount up and get out and don't let us see you in these parts again or you'll end up six feet under with your pardners here," Ned said as he helped the Kid to his feet.

Pulling the Bowie knife from his belt, Ned slashed the Kid's shirt and exposed the wound in his side.

"Don't look too bad, the bullet went clean through," he said, as he made a compress with his neckerchief and pressed it against the wound. "But you're going to be out of commission for a few days. If you want to ride along with us, we'll stop by the Fort and let their Doc patch it up then you can ride in the wagon back to the ranch. A few days rest and you should be good as new; besides, after that draw there's liable to be a few gun slingers in town that would like to try you just to see if that was luck or if you really are that fast. Pulling down on you   might   help to build their reputations as killers."

The Kid smiled and said, "Seems to me you may be a little faster. Could be they might want to try you on for size."

A crowd had gathered at the front of each of the saloons which lined the dirt street, and it was apparent that most of the onlookers were as tough and seedy as this group of gunmen had been. Ned certainly didn't want to get the reputation as a fast draw and have to worry about taking on some of them every time he came to town.

The Kid winced, as Ned pressed his bandana over the hole to stop the blood, and replied. "That's mighty accommodating, Ned. Guess my business in Hidetown is done and I'll be heading back to New Mexico. It's a long ride and a few days rest would do me good. I reckon I'll take you up on your offer."

Sonny and Miguel moved the supplies over to one side in the wagon and made a bed of saddle blankets and helped the Kid into the wagon. The string of horses were tied to the back and they headed out of town, taking the northwest road to Fort Elliot, which lay just over the ridge about a mile.

After stopping at the fort to allow the army surgeon to clean and dress the wound, Ned walked to the fort's Headquarters and asked to speak to the fort's commander, Major James Biddle, who commanded the Sixth Cavalry. Ned had met Major Biddle in Dodge City on their last cattle drive.

"Come in Ned, good to see you again. What can I do for you?"

"Major," Ned responded, nodding his head,"the Colonel sent me over to pick up some supplies and I got caught up in a shooting in Hidetown. Friend of mine took a little lead in the side and your surgeon is working on him. Looks like he might need to stay over for the night and I was just wondering if you'd have any objections to putting us up till morning?"

"Don't see how I can refuse an old army scout and Medal of Honor winner," the Major smiled. "You tell Sergeant Major McClanahan to put you up in the non-commissioned officers quarters and tell the mess sergeant that you'll be eating with us while you are here. I'd be honored if you would have dinner with me and my officers this evening."

"My pleasure, Major."

"We'll be eating at seven."

Ned thanked him, subconsciously gave a limber-wrist salute to the brim of his hat, and walked from the room. Returning to the base hospital, he informed the doctor of his decision to remain at the fort until morning. "I think that's wise, Ned. This boy's wound is not too severe but he lost a lot of blood. He should be able to make the ride without any problems tomorrow," the doctor said, adding, "We'll keep him here in the dispensary until you get ready to leave."

After stowing their plunder in the barracks, Ned asked Sonny and Miguel to tend to the team and keep watch over the Kid until the evening meal when they were to eat with the soldiers. "The Major has asked me to take dinner with him and his officers in the officers' mess. I'll see you later at the barracks."

After a bath and a change of clean clothes, Ned walked to the officers' mess which was on the other side of the parade ground. A young black corporal escorted him into the small dining room where Major Biddle and his contingent of officers were discussing tomorrow's planned activities for the cavalry.

"Come in! Come in, Armstrong!" Biddle shouted, then stepped to the center of the room and placed his arm around Ned's shoulders and said, "Gentlemen, I want you to meet Chief Scout for Colonel Ranald MacKenzie during the Red River Wars. His knowledge of the area was instrumental in the successful campaign to push the recalcitrants back onto the reservations. I might add that he, along with the other six members of the Battle of Buffalo Wallow, was recommended for and awarded the Congressional Medal of Honor. To my knowledge, that was the only battle in the history of our nation when every member involved was so honored."

"Armstrong, I would like for you to meet my officers; Captain Johnson, Adjutant; Lieutenant Beckman, A Company; Lieutenant Woolsey, B Company; Lieutenant McGregor, C Company -- and Captain Peters, our post surgeon who I understand you have already met. Gentlemen, Scout Ned Armstrong!"

Each of the officers stepped by and shook Ned's hand, then offered a toast to the health of the former scout. Ned was embarrassed with the praise being bestowed upon him. He had never considered himself a hero, and for that matter didn't look upon his deeds as bravery, merely as doing the job that he had been hired to do. If anyone was a hero, it was his friend, Billy Dixon. Billy had held the small band together during the battle, and his accuracy with a Winchester had kept the large war party of Cheyennes from overrunning their buffalo wallow position.

As they sat down around the huge table, Colonel Biddle spoke. "Ned, I understand that you are a good friend of Quanah Parker, Chief of the Comanches. Maybe you can tell me whether he's apt to be a problem to us."

"What do you mean, problem?" Ned asked. "Quanah's on the reservation at Fort Sill. How can he cause a problem?"

"There's talk that he might try to slip off the reservation and bring his tribe back and reopen the conflict. With just this one fort to patrol the area, it's going to be hard for us to prevent that from happening."

"You don't have to worry about Quanah, Colonel. He gave his word to me and Colonel Cole, and to Colonel MacKenzie as well, that he would remain on the reservation and try to make a better life for his people. Quanah's word is sacred."

"I'm glad to hear that, Armstrong," Major Biddle replied as he motioned for the men to take their seats around the dinner table.

Since most of the officers were new to the territory, they were anxious to hear Ned's tales of the recent wars with the Indians. They all started asking questions at once.

"Gentlemen," the Major said, "Let Mr. Armstrong eat his dinner, there will be plenty of time after the meal to hear his stories."

After the meal was finished, Major Biddle instructed one of the aides to bring a bottle of his finest whiskey and a box of his best cigars, then asked Ned to tell about his experiences during the recent Indian wars.

Ned, never one to talk much, allowed as how there wasn't much to tell. "Colonel Miles took me on as scout, along with Billy Dixon, Bat Masterson and Amos Chapman, and we just did our jobs the best we knew how."

"There's more to it than that, Armstrong," Biddle said. "Why don't you start at the beginning, when you and Colonel Cole first came into this wild country and made friends with the Indians?"

Ned relaxed and began the story of their friendship with Quanah Parker, how they had become blood brothers after he and Colonel Cole had saved Quanah from quicksand in the Canadian River.

"Guess you must have met old Chief Nocona, Quanah's father," Captain Johnson asked. "They tell me he was a vicious bastard, had a scalp pole long as my leg that was filled up with white men's scalps."

"No, sir," Ned replied. "Well, yes sir, I knew Chief Nocona, but no, sir, he didn't strike me as being vicious. I'd say he was a great chief that did a good job of taking care of his tribe. You got to understand, Captain, this was the Comanche's homeland and what they did, taking scalps and all, was done in trying to protect their land. They trusted me and the Colonel and let us live amongst them in peace. I'd say those scalps you've heard about were probably taken from whites who didn't respect the Comanches' rights."

The officers around the table looked at Ned as if they couldn't believe what he was saying. It was absolutely unthinkable for army personnel to believe that the Indians had any rights.

"After Chief Nocona was killed in the first battle at the old adobe ruins on the Canadian -- that was when Colonel Kit Carson and his cavalry and foot soldiers were nearly massacred by the Comanches, Kiowas, Apaches and Cheyennes -- Quanah was elevated to Chief of the Comanches, and he protected his tribe as well as his father had done," Ned explained. "That was during the summer of '65 when me and the Colonel first started our ranch. Even with the army and the buffalo hunters raising hell with the Indians, Quanah and his tribe continued to treat us as friends."

Seeing that his officers did not agree with Ned's analysis of the Indians, Major Biddle attempted to change the subject. "How did you join up with Colonels Miles and MacKenzie as their scout, Ned."

"That was after the second battle at the old adobe walls ruins on the Canadian, Major, when the buffalo hunters, just twenty-two of 'em, held off over a thousand Indians for two days. During that battle, Colonel Cole got caught with the buffalo hunters and when Quanah discovered he was there, our friendship ended. A couple of weeks later, he led his tribe in an attack on our ranch headquarters. After that, the Colonel and I decided we had to help the army in order to protect our families so I joined up with Colonel Miles as scout, since I knew the area much better than any of his troop."

For two hours, Ned related to the officers of Fort Elliot his exploits as scout with Colonel Miles, and later with Colonel MacKenzie, explaining the terrain which they were going to be patrolling.

As he rose to leave, Major Biddle thanked him for his information and told him that he was welcome at the fort anytime.

"Thanks, Major," Ned replied. "I hope you will visit our ranch, I'm sure Colonel Cole would like to meet you."

Out of habit, he saluted, turned and walked out into the night.

The next morning, Ned and Sonny helped the Kid into the wagon, pulled out of the perimeter of the fort, and headed north following dim wagon tracks towards the valley of the Washita. This was the same trail that he, the Colonel, Belle, Sonny and Miguel had taken the day that Quanah's braves stampeded the buffalo herd down the Sweetwater and over the hundreds of buffalo hunters camps along the stream's banks. Over one hundred of the hunters had been trampled to death that day by the stampeding herd.

The sun was just falling below the caprock as they topped the last rolling hill above Red Deer Creek and looked down upon the huge, rambling ranch house which was the headquarters of the Ceebara spread.

The horses broke into a trot, realizing that they were nearly home. Shep ran down the trail to greet them with a loud bark and the two mules in the nearby corral shattered the evening silence with a loud, piercing bray.

The door to the ranch house opened as they pulled up to the hitching rail, and a tall, one armed man stepped out followed by two beautiful ladies. The man was ex-Confederate Colonel Jim Cole, Ned's partner and father figure. The ladies were Ned's wife Kate and her mother, Belle, who had married the Colonel nearly ten years before.

Kate rushed down the steps and threw her arms around Ned's neck as he dismounted and tied the buckskin to the rail. Ned smiled and kissed her upturned lips, placed his arm around her shoulders and walked her back towards the veranda of the ranch house where Jim and Belle stood watching. A young boy, about ten years old, burst through the door of the ranch house and grabbed Ned by the hand.

Ned squeezed his hand and smiled down at him, "Why don't you look in my saddlebags, Cole," he said, "should be some licorice sticks that Pete sent you."

Then, looking back at the wagon and nodding to Jim, he said, "Brought you a present from Hidetown."

"I see," Jim replied, "looks like a good string of ponies. How'd you come onto them?"

"Wasn't talking about the horses," Ned said in his slow

southern drawl. "Got a wounded cowboy in the wagon."

They stepped quickly from the porch and walked to the wagon where Billy was trying to sit up on the bed of saddle blankets. Sonny and Ramon reached strong arms in and helped him to the ground.

"Kid, this here's my family--Colonel Cole, his wife Belle and my wife Kate. Folks, this is Billy Bonney, but he says just call him Kid."

"Well, Kid, looks like you might have been standing a little too close to some passing lead," Jim said as he shook hands with the wounded stranger. "Come on in the house and tell us what happened."

2

They helped the Kid to a bedroom in the back where Belle cleaned the wound, washed it with drinking whiskey and added a new bandage.

"You get some rest now, boy," she said, "you should feel better tomorrow."

Returning to the front, Ned explained to Jim, Belle and Kate how he had purchased the horses and how the six drifters had tried to steal the horses from him and the Kid.

"I got forced into the fight, Colonel. I never seen those owl hoots before in my life and had no cause for wanting to shoot anybody, they drew and I knew it was either them or me, so I took the Kid's side," Ned said, apologetically.

"Seems to me that's all you could do, under the circumstances, son. I'm just glad that you learned to control that Colt as well as you did. I hope you never have to use it that way again, but if the situation warrants, no one can blame you," Jim said.

"I'll say one thing, Colonel, I've never seen anybody as fast with a gun as the Kid," Ned said, " unless it was you. I just hope I don't ever have to go up against him."

"What do you know about him, Ned? Sounds as if he may be more than just a kid peddling horses. Did you ask where he got the horses?"

"No, sir," Ned replied. "He gave me a bill of sale and I supposed that'd be enough."

"Soon as he gets to feeling better we better find out where he got the horses. We don't want to have stolen stock running with our herd."

* * * * * * *

"I bought 'em from a Mexican trader in Las Vegas, Colonel," Billy said in answer to the question. "A Comanchero trader -- said he picked 'em up down by San Antone. I got no way of knowing if they were stolen or not -- I just know I didn't steal them. He gave me a paper with his X on it saying I bought them from him for two hundred dollars."

"That's good enough for me," Jim replied. "When you mend up, if you want to stick around for awhile, we could use the help -- thirty a month and board."

"I might take you up on that, Colonel, but I need to be getting back to Lincoln before the snows start to blowing. I promised Mr. Chisum I'd ride for him this winter."

"Chisum? Would that be John Chisum from down Waxahatchie way?" Jim asked.

"Yes Sir. He's been over in Lincoln County for the past four years putting together a pretty big spread. I think maybe he's expecting some trouble from some of the local politicians who don't want him taking over land that they consider their own.

"He's an old friend," Jim said, "We rode together before the war -- took a herd from Fort Concho across to the Pecos then up to Colorado and sold them to the army--fought a few Indians along the way but it was worthwhile. That's where I got my stake to buy that ranch down by Austin."

"I'll ride with you, Colonel, if you don't get too riled when I roll up my poke and head back to New Mexico Territory -- I promised Mr. Chisum."

"I understand, Kid -- I like to see a man with loyalty. Always stick to your word and you'll make out O.K."

* * * * * * * *

After a couple of weeks rest, the Kid's wound was healed well enough for him to ride and he began helping with the chores around the ranch.

"Colonel," Ned said, as they were checking the cows which were calving in the Canadian River pasture north of the ranch house, "I'm thinking we best check on the herd grazing the west pasture. Kid said he saw cows carrying our brand nearly all the way to that buffalo hunter's camp at Atascosa Crossing on the Canadian. What with all those damned buffalo hunters roaming that area, some of them might decide cattle rustling would be more profitable than hide hunting. They could round up a thousand head and trail them into Dodge before we'd ever miss them."

"I "spect you're right, Ned. Why don't you take Kid along and check them out. He can point out where he seen them. If they have strayed that far west, the two of you can push them back to the Big Playa pasture. Take one of the mules and pack enough supplies to last you a week or more. Better take along a tarp for cover, you know how these thunderstorms can pop up this time of year."

"Yes, sir, I'll do that. I'll round up Kid and we'll leave at daybreak tomorrow."

* * * * * * * *

Sunup found Ned and the Kid climbing the cut in the cap-rock west of the ranch house, their horses kicking up small rocks as they labored under the climb. The pack mule followed behind, loaded with the supplies for a week's stay on the prairie.

As they rode across the endless miles of tall grass, they were sickened by the sight of the remains of thousands of freshly slaughtered buffalo, bloated bodies with their hides and tongues removed. For as far as they could see in any direction, the bodies lay scattered where the hunters had felled them. Buzzards and coyotes feasted on the grizzly remains, tearing at the stinking flesh and leaving the bones to bleach under the heat of the scorching sun. Bones from last year's kills glistened white among the dark bodies of recent kills, stark witness to the accuracy of the huge buffalo guns.

"Seems like a damned shame," Kid said after they had traveled through miles of the desecration, "One of these days we're going to wake up and they ain't going to be no buffalo left."

"That's what Chief Quanah said the last time we saw him," Ned replied. "It broke his heart and his spirit when he saw what the white man was doing to his land. We tried to stop it, but there were too many hunters and this country is too big for us to police it all. We have been able to keep them away from the herds below the caprock, along the Washita and the Red Deer -- had to use force on some of them but the Colonel enlisted the aid of a couple of the buffalo hunters, Billy Dixon and Bat Masterson, and word was passed to the hunters that this herd is off limits. The Colonel plans to invite Quanah's tribe for a hunt each year until they are able to adjust to the white man's ways. General MacKenzie has sent word that he is agreeable to allow them to participate in a hunt."

This had been a good year for rain and the grass was tall and green. Playa lakes scattered over the area were holding water and as they rode slowly west, they began to see small herds of magnificent longhorns grazing on the lush grass, scattered across the endless plains. After two days ride, Ned allowed as how they had reached the western edge of the Ceebara property, which was listed on the land grant papers as being *a north-south line from the Canadian River to the headwaters of the North Fork of the Red River.*

Many cattle could be seen west of that line so they continued their journey towards Atascosa Crossing on the Canadian, where a small community had sprung up as a result of the buffalo hunters invading the plains. Dodge City buyers had even sent freighters to the small hunters' camp to purchase the hides and haul them back to the railroad for shipment back east.

Dropping off into the Canadian River breaks, Ned pulled his horse to a stop and motioned for the Kid to do the same, placing his finger over his lips as a sign to be quiet. Listening, they could hear a strange sound coming from around one of the small buttes which dotted the area.

Ned, looking at the Kid, asked, "What"s that noise?"

"Sounds like sheep," Kid replied.

"Sheep? Ain't no sheep in this country!"

"If it ain't sheep, then you got some cows with an awful peculiar sounding bawl."

They rode slowly around the edge of the butte and sure enough, there was a huge herd of sheep grazing lazily towards the river. Off to the right was a strange looking wagon with a canvas top and a stove pipe sticking out of the middle. Two men were standing by the wagon and two huge sheep dogs were slowly circling the herd, keeping them all in a bunch.

"*Buenos Dias*," one of the men said as Ned and Kid approached.

"*Buenos Dias,*" Ned replied. "*Como este borregos.*"

Ned's understanding of Spanish was minimal, having picked up a few words and phrases from the Garcia family who had accompanied him and Colonel Cole from Central Texas to the Panhandle, in 1866, when they brought their herd of longhorns up the trail. It was limited to what had become known as Tex-Mex. He hoped the Mexican could understand that he wished to know where the hell these sheep had come from.

To Ned's surprise, Kid spoke fluent Spanish, and after a short discussion with the sheepherder, he turned to Ned and explained that the man's name was Romero, and he had trailed his sheep along the Canadian from New Mexico Territory. The border between Texas and New Mexico was only about fifty miles to the west. Other Mexican families had come with him and had their sheep herds scattered along the river and up on the plains farther west. As near as he could tell, there must be twenty or thirty thousand head of sheep in the area.

"The Mexicans have built several plazas along the river and his plaza is located at Atascosa Crossing," Kid said.

Ned couldn't believe what he was hearing. "The Colonel ain't going to like this one danged bit," he said, "this ain't sheep country, it's cow country. You tell these *hombres* that Ceebara property starts just over that ridge and we don't want any sheep eating our grass."

Kid explained to the Mexicans about the Ceebara ranch and that sheep would not be welcome any farther east.

"*Si, senor,*" Romero said, then in broken English, he added, "We will keep our *carneros* west of your ranchero, maybe so you will keep your *vacas* east of *our* grazing lands."

Ned smiled, the Mexican had him there, this was no-man's land and the sheep men had just as much right to graze their herds as the cow men had a right to graze their cattle.

"*Bueno, Senor* Romero, we will try to keep our cattle away from your sheep," he said, smiling.

"Maybe you have more cattle ranchers that don't like *carneros* here on the *Llano Estacado,*" Romero said, more as a statement than as a question.

"No," Ned answered, "Ceebara is the only ranch and our cattle are the only cattle for many miles in any direction."

"That is not so, *Senor,*" the Mexican replied. "This morning we met a man with many longhorn cattle from Colorado who said he was taking the cattle to the big canyon to the south where he is starting a ranch. The man said his name was Goodnight, and like you, he asked that we keep our *carneros* away from his ranch."

"Where is this man and his herd?" Ned asked, disbelieving.

"Maybe ten miles to the south. If you ride back on top of the plains to the southwest you will see his trail."

Turning to Kid, Ned said, "Ain't no cattle on these plains but Ceebara cattle. If Romero saw a cow herd then it must be rustlers taking a cut out of our herd!"

"*Senor*," Romero said when he saw that Ned was upset about other cattlemen being in the area, "That is not all. I have seen signs of many cattle in the canyons north and west of my Plaza on the river. Maybe you have more neighbors who like this country for their cattle."

Ned thanked him and spurred the buckskin into a lope in the direction indicated by Romero. It was almost unbelievable -- sheep and now another herd of cattle invading their territory, if in fact, Romero was right. And cattle north of the river? No telling what was going to happen next, with the Indians all gone, squatters would probably be swarming in and plowing up the grass like Quanah had predicted. *The Colonel just ain't going to like this at all,* he thought.

"*Adios, Amigo*," the Kid shouted to Romero as he spurred his bay in an effort to catch up with Ned who had disappeared around the lip of the small butte.

Romero waved and shouted back, "*Adios -- Vaya con Dios.*"

The trail of the herd was not hard to find, and Ned and the Kid were soon following it southeast across the prairie where the grass had been trampled by two or three thousand head of cattle. Ned, watching the ground closely, determined that there were eight horsemen driving the herd with two wagons trailing behind.

They saw the dust cloud first, then the white sheet of the wagons reflecting the sun, then the dark objects of the cow herd stretched out ahead of the wagons.

"I 'spect we'd best circle around them so I can put my glass on the tail end of the herd and check for our brand before we go busting in on them," Ned said as he turned his horse to the east and pushed him into a fast trot.

They rode in that direction for about fifteen minutes before turning back, parallel to the herd. Another hour and they had passed the wagons and could see the broad side of the stragglers being pushed by the drag riders. Ned pulled his horse to a stop and reached in his saddle bag for the small telescope which he always carried with him.

Adjusting it, he slowly moved it from the wagons to the head of the herd and counted eight horsemen and two wagon drivers. Stopping the movement of the glass, he gazed intently at the side of one of the nearest cows. The C Bar A brand was not present on the left hip! Looking closely, he could see a 'C G' branded on the left shoulder.

Charles Goodnight! So Romero had been right, this was not Ceebara cattle but a new herd being brought into the area. Ned handed the telescope to the Kid as he said, "Looks like Romero was right, them ain't our cows. See if that ain't a C G brand on the left shoulder."

"Sure as hell is," Kid replied, "and I don't see any sign of the Ceebara brand on the hip. Guess these fellers are fixing to stake them out a claim on some of this prairie grass."

He returned the glass to Ned who replaced it in the saddlebag, before kicking his horse into a lope and headed for the wagons.

"Howdy," the chuck wagon driver shouted as Ned rode up. "Didn't reckon as how they was any white folks within four hundred miles of us," he said as he spit a brown stream of tobacco juice onto the wheel of the wagon.

"Them's my sentiments, exactly," Ned replied. "Who's the boss of this herd?"

"They call me Hard Tack," the driver answered. "I'm the cook. The boss is Colonel Goodnight and he's up yonder at the head of this mangy bunch of horns, where I'd be if'n I hadn't had some trouble with my wagon. I'm just now catching up to the herd but I'm going to go around them and get back up front out of this consarned dust --" Spitting another stream and wiping the drippings from his long handle-bar mustache before completing his statement, "that's the Colonel on the big blue roan."

"Much obliged, Hard Tack. My name's Ned and my pardner just goes by Kid," Ned said as he kicked the buckskin into a trot and headed for the front of the herd.

Goodnight saw them coming and pulled to the side and let the herd pass as he waited for them to ride up.

"Howdy, gents," he said as Ned and Kid pulled their horses to a halt, nose to nose with his roan.

He was a bull of a man, about forty years old, Ned calculated. His hair was long with a sprinkling of gray around the edges and he wore a full beard which was trimmed but growing, witness to several days on the trail. A large, black, straight-brimmed hat topped his head and he was dressed in typical cowman clothes. Although there was a Winchester rifle shoved into the boot of the saddle, he wore no guns at his waist.

"Name's Ned Armstrong, Mr. Goodnight, and this here's Billy Bonney who works for me and Colonel Jim Cole."

"Another Colonel, 'eh," Goodnight said, smiling, "that's what most folks call me -- *Colonel* -- but it's more of an honorary name because of my work with the Texas Rangers."

"Yes, sir," Ned replied. "Colonel Cole is a real 'un, fought in the Confederacy under General Lee. Me and him met on the battlefield after a canon ball took off his arm and danged near killed him. I did what I could to keep him from bleeding to death and ever since he's treated me like I was his own son."

"Well, Ned, looks to me like he might have made a pretty good choice," Goodnight replied, smiling. "I take it Hard Tack told you my name, glad to meet you boys. What brings you out here in the middle of nowhere?"

"Well, Sir, it ain't the middle of nowhere. Just to the east a few miles is the west property line of the Ceebara ranch which belongs to the Colonel and me -- and I was just about to ask what you was doing out here with a herd of mangy longhorns. Seems this country is getting downright crowded with Mexican sheep herders and Colorado cowboys cluttering it up."

Goodnight laughed, "Well, young feller, looks to me like there's enough grass to go around, but I ain't aiming to stop for awhile. I scouted out a big canyon last year forty or fifty miles ahead and that's where we're headed. Figured I'd set roots in the bottom of that canyon and spend the rest of my days on this here earth just building one of the best cow ranches in the southwest."

Stepping off his horse, he walked stiffly to Ned's horse and shoved his big hand up in greeting. Ned accepted it in a friendly handshake and smiled as he dismounted. Ned was nearly as tall as Goodnight, but not as heavy. Looking into Goodnight's eyes, he could see a glint of kindness, but also a hint of toughness -- one that said *I'll be your friend but I'll expect the same from you.*

"Seems I heard something about a ranch over east along the Canadian but didn't realize it was this far west," he said. "Didn't mean to crowd you up none, but with the Indians corralled, I expect there's going to be a lot of us cowmen laying claim to this grass where we can run our cows." Smiling, he added, "and maybe a few sheepmen."

"I expect so, sir," Ned replied, "but I hope they respect our property lines. We been working our tails off for ten years to establish our herd and build our boundaries. We fought Indians, buffalo hunters and even the army to get our roots set. I hope we don't have to fight other cattlemen now to keep what is ours."

"You won't have any trouble with me, son,"Goodnight replied. "You just tell me where your property lines are and I'll respect them. Didn't know I was going to have neighbors, but I intend to be a good one."

"Well, sir, I guess there's enough grass for all of us. The legislature of the Republic of Texas made a land grant to the Colonel away back in 1844 -- due to the prodding of General Sam Houston -- but he never had a chance to prove up on it until after the war, when me and him came up and staked it out. The grant papers describe it with the east boundary being a north-south line from the Canadian River to the North Fork of the Red River at the head of the Sweetwater Creek, then west up the North Fork of the Red River to it's head, then back north on a north-south line to the Canadian River, then east down the Canadian back to the east line. The Colonel says there's probably a million acres or more."

Goodnight whistled, then said, "That's a powerful lot of grass, boy -- going to take a lot of cattle to fill it up."

"Yes, sir. We brought up five thousand head from Central Texas ten years ago and we been building a herd ever since. We've made several drives to Dodge City to market our steers, but we've kept all the cows and heifers. I calculate we got nigh onto twenty-five thousand head scattered over these plains today."

Goodnight whistled again before replying, then said, "Well, ain't that something! And I thought I was going to have these plains all to myself." Then removing his hat and scratching his head, he added, "Ten years? How in tarnation did you manage to keep from losing your hair to the Comanches -- I thought they controlled this area?"

"They did, Colonel, but we made friends with Chief Nocona and his son Quanah. Fact is, Quanah made us his blood brothers after we saved him from quicksand on the Canadian and he kinda kept the other tribes off our backs. We left their buffalo alone and they didn't bother our cattle and we didn't have any Indian problems at all until the buffalo hunters came in and started taking hides."

"I guess when the army came in and started pushing the

tribes back onto the reservations you was caught in the middle, wasn't you, Ned?"

"Yes, sir. It got pretty rough when the Indian wars began. The Colonel was caught with a bunch of buffalo hunters at Adobe Walls along with Billy Dixon and Bat Masterson. Quanah thought he was taking the hunter's side in the war and that was the end of our friendship for awhile. Colonel Miles hired me on as scout after that and I was with him and Colonel MacKenzie when the last tribes were herded back to the reservation."

"I heard the last battle was fought down in the Palo Duro where I'm headed. Was you there?" Goodnight asked.

"Yes, sir. Me and Billy Dixon showed Colonel MacKenzie where the trail was located that the Indians used to get down into the canyon from up here on top of the plains. I don't know if you heard the story how the Indians kinda forted up behind the rocks and canyons and Colonel MacKenzie decided to just burn their lodges and take all their horses and supplies and leave them there. He figured they would have to slip back to the reservation or freeze and starve with winter coming on. We trailed their horses back up to the top and drove them about thirty miles south to the head of Tule Canyon where the Colonel's wagons were waiting. I couldn't believe it, but Colonel MacKenzie ordered his troops to kill all those Indian ponies -- must have been over a thousand head -- so they wouldn't slip back and steal them at night."

"I heard about it -- seems terrible to treat good horse flesh that way. But I guess that's war--wasn't any use in him taking a chance that the Indians would get them horses back, it would just mean another battle," Goodnight commented.

"Yes, Sir -- but you know, I never could understand why Colonel MacKenzie didn't just shoot them horses down in the bottom of the canyon instead of going to the trouble of herding them up on top and then driving them another thirty miles before killing them."

The tail end of the herd passed and Goodnight started to remount, then paused. Looking at Ned he said, "Sounds to me like you know this area just about as good as your Comanche friends. Reckon I could persuade you to ride along with us and show me where that trail is that leads into the canyon? I've been at a loss trying to figure how I'm going to get these horns down that cliff."

"I'd like to help, Colonel, but we got cattle straying too far off our range and Kid and me came out to push them back towards headquarters. Might take us four or five days the way they are scattered."

Goodnight thought for a minute, then replied. "My scout told me there's a playa with plenty of water in it about two hours ahead. This herd needs a rest -- why don't we stop for a couple of days and let them graze and I'll send my boys along with you and help push your strays back onto your property. With the extra help you should be able to get them back in a couple of days then you could ride along with me and show me that trail. I sure would be much obliged."

Ned welcomed the idea of additional help and was quick to agree. Goodnight's herd was probably no more than two days drive from the head of the canyon and he calculated that they could do both jobs and still get back to headquarters before the family started worrying about him.

After the herd was watered at the playa and Hard Tack had

prepared a supper of buffalo roast and beans, the crew sat a-round the buffalo chip fire and listened to Ned tell about his experiences during the past ten years.

"After MacKenzie had the Indian ponies shot, I figured my work as scout was finished so I headed back to Ceebara headquarters," he said. He didn't tell how Quanah had been wounded and captured in the battle of the Palo Duro, and how he had helped the Comanche chief, his wife, Morning Star, and their young son, Jim Bold Eagle to escape from MacKenzie's troop. He figured the least said about that episode the better.

"Quanah was able to gather most of his tribe back together and they walked the eighty miles back to Ceebara headquarters where we fed them and let them remain through the winter. The next spring, Quanah led them to Fort Sill where they turned themselves in. It's my understanding that Quanah was the only chief who was not tried and sent to prison in Florida. Seems MacKenzie learned that Quanah's tribe had never signed any peace treaties, therefore they were not guilty of breaking the treaties. Last I heard, MacKenzie was using Quanah to lead most of the tribes on the reservation and that he had become as good a leader for peace as he had been a leader in war."

Goodnight listened intently as Ned spun his tale, then asked, "Sounds to me like you and the Colonel don't think too highly of buffalo hunters. How come?"

"Well, sir, if the buffalo hunters hadn't started slaughtering all the herds, we never would have had trouble with the Indians. But that wasn't the main reason. Some of the hunters were real fine folks, just trying to make a living, like Billy

Dixon and Bat Masterson. But most were mean as hell! One bunch of them pert near killed the Colonel and raped his wife, Belle, out here on the prairie. Belle is my mother-in-law -- I married her daughter. If it hadn't been for Quanah and some of his braves coming on them at just the right time, I 'spect both of them would be dead. The Indians killed the hunters and carried Belle and the Colonel back to their camp and nursed them back to health. So you see, we owe Quanah and the Comanches a lot."

Goodnight nodded his head sadly. "I can see why you feel the way you do. Looks to me like you folks could trust the Indians more than you could trust the buffalo hunters."

"Yes, Sir," Ned replied. "Most of them, that is. Now, Billy Dixon and Bat Masterson were different. They respected our range and when the Colonel asked them not to take hides on Ceebara property, they obliged. Fact is, they became real good friends and I rode side by side with them as scouts for MacKenzie's cavalry. They drop by the ranch ever now and again for a visit. Like most of the hunters, they bring their hides into Hidetown to sell and it's just a day's ride on over to our headquarters."

As Ned finished his story, the cowboys backed away from the glowing coals of the fire and spread their bedrolls, pulled their blankets over their bodies and drifted off to sleep, realizing that there was a lot of riding to do tomorrow, gathering the Ceebara strays and pushing them back onto the ranch.

Although Ned's body was totally exhausted, his mind continued to rehash the day's events as he lay on his bedroll listening to the snores of the other cowboys. There was a nagging thought that continued to keep him awake. Why had his cattle strayed so far from the ranch with good grass and plenty of water to keep them satisfied when they had never strayed before? And now that he thought about it, he had noticed too many doggie calves without mamas along with the strays.

And Romero had said there were signs of other cattle north of the river. That just didn't make sense. As sleep finally took over, his last thoughts were that he was going to need to check out the accuracy of Romero's story about more cattle north of the river.

3

Soon after Ned and the Kid had left ranch headquarters, Jim and Belle were riding in the Canadian river pasture, checking cows which were calving. The weather was perfect, a few cumulus clouds floating overhead, very little wind and the temperature hovering around seventy degrees.

"Jim, it's times like this makes me realize that all the hardships in making our ranch have been worth it. God surely worked overtime to paint such a beautiful picture as this. Look at those baby calves, spotted with most of the colors of the rainbow, frolicking in that tall green grass. And their mamas, fat and slick with those huge horns glistening in the sunshine," Belle said.

Pointing to the west, Jim answered, "And look at those tan and white antelopes, grazing with that small herd of black, shaggy buffalo. And over there, that bunch of buffalo, grazing with those longhorn cattle. God not only paints a pretty picture, he also knows how to create peace among the races -- something we have yet to learn."

Letting his gaze lift above the grazing herds, Jim glanced across the Canadian River and saw several hundred head of longhorns, trailing towards the river for water.

"Now how do you suppose those cattle got across that river without bogging in the quicksand? We best check them out, Belle, there may be some bogged that we can't see from here," Jim said as he spurred the big black stallion towards the river.

Belle followed on her roan mare.

Reaching the bank of the river, Jim rode downstream until he found a likely place to cross and urged the stallion into the water. The water was only stirrup deep and the two horses splashed across to the north side without any problem.

The longhorns were now scattered along the north bank of the river, heads lowered and taking their fill of the clear river water.

Jim rode close to one of the more gentle cows and Belle heard him exclaim, "Would you look at that! These ain't our cows, they got a brand on the left hip that looks like a quarter circle over a T. Must be some that strayed all the way down from Dodge City last winter during one of the blizzards. Look yonder, there's some more up there on top of the caprock.

Sure enough, another bunch was beginning to appear on the lip of the caprock and were descending to the river through a small cut in the cliff.

Jim spurred the black in that direction and the cattle scattered as he urged the stallion up the trail to the top. Reaching the top, he was amazed to see several hundred more grazing a mile or so to the north. As he loped by them he could see they were all carrying the *Quarter Circle T* brand.

As Belle pulled her mare up beside him, she pointed towards a small column of smoke, rising from a canyon off to their left,. Jim nodded and turned the black in that direction.

Another half mile, and they were on the edge of the small, protected canyon, looking down on the top of a half-dugout cabin. Two horses were tied to a hitching rail in front of the dugout, lazily switching flies with their tails. Six more head were standing, three-legged in a small corral back of the dugout, dozing in the warm sunshine of this carefree, spring day. Their eyes opened and their ears perked forward when they realized that strangers were approaching from the hill behind the house. All six nickered a welcome.

Fifty yards east of the house, two sheet-covered wagons were parked next to a long lean-to, made with cedar posts and covered with brush for a top. Several bedrolls were scattered about, similar to a cattle drive campground.

A woman stepped from the door of the dugout and threw a wash pan of water into the yard. A half dozen White Leghorn hens scattered as the water splashed towards where they had been scratching in the sand. A Dominaker rooster fluffed his feathers and made as if he would attack the water thrower, before he too, headed for the protection of the horse corral.

Seeing the two riders approaching, she turned towards the door and Jim could hear her shout, "Mr. Bugbee, strangers are a'comin down the trail. Better git yourself out here!"

Immediately, a tall, raw-boned man appeared in the doorway, levering a shell into the chamber of a Winchester rifle. He stepped three paces away from the woman who had retreated to the cabin door, and stood with the rifle held loosely in the crook of his arm, the other hand clamped firmly around the trigger guard. The barrel of the rifle was pointed in the direction of the approaching riders.

"Howdy," the man with the rifle said, as Jim pulled the

black to a stop, ten paces in front of the dugout.

"Howdy," Jim responded as Belle pulled the roan to a stop next to Jim's horse. Glancing at the woman, Jim touched the brim of his hat and nodded politely.

"Weren't expectin no company, seeing as how we ain't been in these parts very long. Didn't allow as how anyone knew we was here. Name's Bugbee, Tom Bugbee and this here's my wife, Molly," the man said.

"Jim Cole, Mr. Bugbee, and this is my wife, Belle. I reckon as how we're about as surprised as you, seeing that we weren't expecting to find any white folks in these parts."

"Lordy, me!" Molly said, wiping her hands on her apron. "Lordy, me! A woman! I ain't seen another woman since we left Dodge City with this herd of longhorns over two months ago. Where's your manners Mr. Bugbee, ask these folks down off them horses and invite them in for coffee. Lordy, me! I don't believe it, we got female company!"

"Molly's right, dag-nab it, light off them horses and come in and set awhile and tell us what you're doing in these parts," Bugbee said, leaning the rifle against the wall of the dugout, then walking towards Jim with his hand outstretched and a smile on his face.

Jim and Belle dismounted and Jim took Tom's outstretched right hand in his left and shook it awkwardly. When Tom stared at the empty right sleeve, Jim smiled and said simply, "Lost it to canon grape during the war."

Belle walked towards Molly and the two women reached out to each other, taking each other's hands. Molly held onto Belle as if afraid she might only be a figment of her imagination--afraid that she might disappear at any minute.

"Lordy, me!" she said once more, almost in a whisper with a tear showing in each eye.

Although beautiful this time of year, the *Llano Estacado* in 1876 was a lonely place in which to live. Now with the Indians pushed back into Indian Territory, a person could travel for days across these trackless grasslands without setting eyes on another human being--especially another white, female human being. So no wonder that Molly was so excited to see Belle.

Tom Bugbee held the door open while the two ladies and Jim entered the dugout. Only one large room, it was sparsely furnished with handmade furniture. A large table was in the center of the room with a coal oil lamp burning brightly on its top. The two windows were covered with buffalo hide curtains, making the lamp necessary even during the day.

The walls of the crude home were sand rock, cut and placed together as brick. The floor was dirt and the roof was cottonwood and hackberry logs covered with thick layers of prairie sod.

In the back of the room, a rough rock fireplace had been built with a flue extending through the roof. The fireplace served as a furnace as well as a cook stove, with andirons and a long, steel, horizontal rod extending across the middle which held hanging cast iron pots over the hearth. A bed of coals glowed brightly in the dim light of the room. One of the pots was simmering with boiling coffee which filled the room with the familiar aroma of the strong brew.

A rough bed with a feather mattress and quilts was on one side of the room and wooden pegs lined the walls where clothes were hung.

"Sit down! Sit down!" Tom said as he pointed to the benches on either side of the table.

Molly continued to stand in awe, looking at Belle as if she couldn't believe she was having visitors, wringing her hands together.

"Molly!" Tom shouted, bringing her out of her reverie. "Pour our friends some coffee."

"Oh, I'm so sorry," she said to Belle. "I was so excited that you are here, I clean forgot my manners," as she rushed to the fireplace, lifted the blackened coffee pot and poured four cups which were already on the rough table.

Jim and Belle sat at the table as Tom took their hats and hung them on wall pegs.

"You folks just traveling through?" Tom asked, and before Jim could answer, added, "Looks like you're traveling mighty light--nothing but bedrolls and slickers on your hosses."

"No, Tom, I guess you could say we're your neighbors. We got a spread south of the river. Been here building our ranch for the past ten years. We got a ranch house and headquarters just over the ridge on Red Deer Creek, maybe thirty miles. Me and Belle were out checking our cows when we saw your herd across the river -- thought it might be ours so we came over to investigate. Didn't have no idea that you folks had moved into the area."

Tom was amazed, "A ranch? Just thirty miles away! Now ain't that something, Molly!" Turning his eyes from his wife back to Jim, he added, "We never thought they was any white folks in this country closer than Dodge City."

"Shows how wrong a person can be, Tom. You must have

come in from the north, otherwise you'd have seen our sign. We got cows scattered over nigh onto a million acres across the river, mostly up on top of the plains this time of year," Jim explained.

"Yes, sir, we did come in from the north. Me and Molly had a spread up in Kansas but Indians kept pestering us so much we decided to move down here after we heard the army had pushed the red skins back onto the reservations. Me and Molly and five cowhands trailed in about eighteen hundred head of cows, and decided the grass was so good along the Canadian that this is where we'd stake our claim. We just got this diggin's finished a couple of weeks ago. Spect it'll keep us out of the weather this winter, and next spring we plan on building a house a little farther to the north."

Taking a sip of his coffee, Tom looked at Jim almost in awe and asked, "A million acres -- you intend to lay claim to a million acres of this grass? That's going to take a goshawful lot of cattle to stock it right."

Jim placed his cup down and nodded, "Yep, a million acres. Except I don't have to lay claim to it, the Republic of Texas granted it to me in 1844, before Texas became a state in 1845. The General--Sam Houston, that is--was like a daddy to me and he got the legislature to make me the grant. Nobody was really interested in this part of the country back then, thought it wasn't no good for anything except rattlesnakes and wild Indians. Texas was mostly divided up into huge Spanish land grants back then, so it wasn't any problem to get them to grant some of this country to any fool that was willing to come up and try to settle it, while fighting off the Comanches and Cheyennes."

Tom laughed, then asked, "Ten years ago, you say. How'd you manage to do it when there weren't no white folks up here, just you and the injuns?"

"Lucky, I guess," Jim answered, then told the Bugbees about their experiences with the Indians. "Guess we've got about twenty-five thousand head grazing these plains today," he added.

Tom whistled. "Twenty-five thousand! Hear that, Molly. We thought we had a pretty good herd, just under two thousand. Maybe ten years from now, we'll run that many."

"It don't take long," Jim said, "If you keep all the heifers and don't sell any cows. We been trailing all our three year old steers up to Dodge for the past five or six years for shipment to the markets back east, but we don't sell any female stock."

They continued to sit around the table, visiting and enjoying each others company until the sun began to reach the western horizon. Jim pulled himself up from the bench, reaching for his hat which was hung on a peg on the wall. "Reckon we'd best be on our way, Belle," he said, "we got just about enough time to reach that campground on the other side of the river before dark."

Molly looked to Tom, questioningly and Tom spoke. "We ain't going to hear to it, Jim. These diggin's ain't much, but they beat hell out of sleeping in the open. Besides, looks like a thunderstorm building back to the west--liable to rain afore morning. We want you folks to spend the night with us. I've got a passel of questions I want to ask and I know Molly's hankering to find out more about your ranch house and the rest of your family. I sent my hands back to Dodge City with a couple of wagons to bring in supplies for winter, so they ain't no one here but me and Molly. You just pull your bed rolls off them hosses and bring them inside. Whilst Molly and Belle rustle up some grub, we'll take your mounts down to the corrals and throw them some hay and a bait of oats."

Jim looked at Belle and she nodded her head in agreement. "Well, that's real neighborly, Tom. I guess we could wait 'till morning to head back. Kate's not expecting us back before tomorrow, anyways, and Ned's still off up west, pushing strays back onto our grass. We kinda got worried that some of these buffalo hunters might decide to take up ranching, using our cows as foundation stock since the buffalo herds are beginning to peter out."

Tom laughed. "That's a pretty nice way to call them rustlers, Jim. But I wouldn't put it past them. Me and Molly been talking about the same thing. With this wide open country, and no more help than we've got, they could run off half our herd and have them shipped out of Dodge before we would know they was gone."

* * * * * * * *

Dutch Henry, former buffalo hunter and veteran of the Adobe Walls battle along with Billy Dixon, Bat Masterson and Jim Cole, had taken up residence in Hidetown. He liked the wild and rough life associated with the numerous saloons and bawdy houses of the frontier town--and the fact that no lawman had taken up residence in the area. Many of the town's *painted ladies* were acquainted with the big hunter's antics in their bedrooms and his brawls in the saloons. Most of his hide money found warmth between the covers of their feather beds.

As the buffalo herds along the Canadian began to diminish, Dutch began to look for other means to fill his pockets with enough gold to satisfy his wants and desires. Taking along some of his skinners and a few gun slingers who had taken up residence in the Sodom of the Plains, Dutch decided to share his needs with some of the more affluent Dodge City merchants who were sending wagon trains down the Ceebara Trail to Hidetown, carrying supplies and gold with which to purchase the buffalo hunters' hides.

Riding in during the early morning hours along the Canadian River, while the members of the wagon trains were still asleep, Dutch and his highwaymen would wake them with six-guns pointed at their heads and demand the gold which was to be used to purchase hides. Very few of the freighters had nerve enough to refuse to obey Dutch's demands.

Such activities were sufficient for a while to keep enough money in the notorious outlaw's pockets to satisfy his needs in Hidetown. However, the merchants were quick to send armed guards along with the freight wagons, and on one early morning attack, three of the outlaws were killed. Dutch began to look for safer means of work.

Noticing the thousands of longhorns grazing the plains with very few cowboys looking after them, he formulated a plan to start his own cattle business.

* * * * * * * *

With the additional help of Goodnight and his cowboys,

Ned and the Kid made quick work of pushing their strays back onto Ceebara grass. He was concerned and puzzled that several dogie calves, calves with no mamas, were a part of the strays. He voiced his concern to the Kid as they sat their horses, resting and rolling a smoke.

"Kid, did ya notice that a bunch of them calves is about starved, don't seem to have no mamas?"

"Couldn't help but notice them, Ned. Must be thirty or forty. I 'spect they'll be able to make it though, most of them are old enough to eat grass."

Ned placed the cigarette in his mouth, pulled a match from his shirt pocket and struck it on his saddle horn. He inhaled and blew the smoke before voicing his thoughts.

"I'm not too concerned about whether they make it or not. I'm sure you're right. What I cain't figure is what happened to their mamas. We haven't seen any dead cattle, just dead buffalo scattered all over the area. I suppose the cattle could have been stampeded by the buffalo hunters and the calves got separated from the cows, but we've had buffalo hunters shooting amongst our cattle for a couple of years now, and this is the first time I've noticed so many bum calves."

Kid finished rolling his smoke, lit it and as if talking to himself, said, "maybe they didn't have to stampede 'em. Maybe they took a liking to 'em."

Ned looked at him and smiled. "You may be right, Kid. I spect we'd best check that out when we get Colonel Goodnight's herd down in the canyon." He kicked the buckskin in the side and turned him back towards the Goodnight herd.

* * * * * * * *

It wasn't much of a camp. An area cleaned off under one of the huge cottonwood trees where rocks had been piled in a circle, forming a crude fireplace. Smoke curled from the glowing coals and a huge cast iron coffee pot hung from a steel rod which had been fitted between the forks of two cottonwood limbs at either end of the fire.

A half dozen cowboys lay around in the shade, dozing in the noonday heat, heads resting on their saddles which had been thrown haphazardly around the camp. A rope corral had been strung between several of the trees next to the spring and about twenty head of horses stood swatting flies with their tails. Now and again, they would stomp their feet and ripple their skin to put a deer fly to flight which had been sucking blood from areas safe from the switching tails.

Dutch Henry walked to the fire, removed the coffee pot and poured a tin cupful, took a sip of the steaming brew as he watched another group of cowboys coming up the canyon, herding about fifty head of longhorns before them.

"That's Ringo and Cheyenne, Boss. They're the last ones. Everyone else is in," the tall, slim wrangler called Rusty said, as he took the pot and poured himself a cup.

As they approached, Dutch shouted orders. "Just head 'em up the canyon where we got the others grazing," he told the first cowboy, "then come back and have some of this coffee. We'll put our mark on 'em first thing in the morning.

"Tater will have us some steaks cooking pretty soon," he added as he pointed to a tall, skinny cowhand who was cutting steaks off the hind quarter of a dressed-out steer hanging from the branches of one of the trees. The hide, thrown on the ground below the beef, clearly showed the C Bar A brand.

The cowhand pushing the newly arrived cattle nodded without speaking as he headed the herd past the campground.

A thousand or more cows and steers were leisurely grazing along the small stream no more than a quarter of a mile from the camp. When the newly arrived herd saw them, they began to bawl and struck a trot to join the larger group. The cowboys turned their horses and returned to the camp.

"That makes close to eleven hundred head," Dutch said, speaking to the nearest cowhand, a large dark skinned man with a crooked nose and a face covered with a thick black beard. "I 'spect that soon's we get 'em marked, we best head them west into New Mexico Territory. Once we get them out of Texas, we'll turn them north up towards the Rabbit Ears, rest them up and let their hair grow, then, just before winter, we can head them back east to Dodge City without running into any of Cole's cowhands."

"Every one of them damned longhorns has got that C BAR A brand on their left hip, boss," the large man with the crooked nose said. "All them buyers in Dodge City are going to know who they belong to and won't touch them with a ten foot pole. How you planning on getting them sold?"

"Ain't going to be C Bar A cattle when they get to Dodge. We've been doing a little experimenting with a running iron; it's going to be real easy to change that C into an O, make a cross out of the bar, and blot the A to where it looks like a triangle. After we finish our branding, these 'horns are going to belong to a new ranch in the Texas Panhandle--the Circle-Cross-Triangle. After a couple months of new hair growing over the brand, no one can tell the difference."

Pausing, he took a sip of the black coffee, took a drag on his cigarette and blew the smoke out his nose as he gazed at the herd which was grazing about a half mile up the canyon.

"Eleven hundred head at forty dollars a head is going to fetch us a pocket full of gold," he said to no one in particular. "That'd be nigh onto fifty thousand dollars! That'll buy us a heap of whiskey and keep them painted up ladies in the Long Branch and the Lady Gay busy all winter long!"

Rusty smacked his lips and laughed at the thought.

* * * * * * * *

Ned and Colonel Goodnight rode ahead of the herd as it approached the Palo Duro. The flat terrain of the plains suddenly dropped off into a shallow valley, where a small, clear stream cut through its middle.

"The Indian trail down the side of the canyon is over yonder," he told Goodnight, pointing to the south. "Probably no more'n four or five miles. We probably should stop the herd here until morning."

"Fine, Ned, we'll bed them down here, let them drink and graze, and try to push them down in the morning."

"It's going to be a job, Colonel, that trail is hardly wide enough for a horse and rider--them cows are going to have a tough time making it with their six feet wide horns."

"I think we can get Old Blue to try it, Ned. The other cows will follow him into hell if he will just open the trail."

Leaving the herd behind, they rode up to the brink of the canyon just as the sun was reaching the western horizon. The colors below them were dazzling. Looking across the huge

51

chasm, they could see the bright white caprock on the other side reflecting the sun's rays. Below it, the reds of the clays, the blues of the shales and the whites of the gypsums blended into the greens of the canyon's floor. Far below, a tiny ribbon of blue meandered down the canyon to the south--the headwaters of the Prairie Dog Town Fork of the Red River. Huge cottonwoods lined the banks of the clear stream, and a large herd of buffalo could be seen wading and drinking along its banks. A half dozen Bald Eagles circled lazily overhead.

As they watched, the floor of the canyon began to darken as the sun's rays were blotted out by the canyon's rim. Looking across the canyon, the colors on the face of the wall began to change colors as the angle of the setting sun became greater and greater. The layers of gypsum began to reflect the gold of the sun's rays -- and blues, greys and reds became richer and darker in color.

"Ain't that a sight to behold, Ned?" the Colonel said. "God never made a more perfect place for a ranch."

"Yes, sir," Ned responded as he took in the splendor of the moment. "But I 'spect God never intended for fools such as us to try to get two thousand head of mangy longhorns down these cliffs, either."

Goodnight laughed.

They turned their horses back towards the herd which had taken its fill of water and was scattered out along the small stream's edge, grazing on the knee high prairie grass. As they rode up, the aroma of fresh coffee greeted them--Hard Tack had already made camp and was cooking steaks and beans over a buffalo chip fire.

Sitting around the campfire eating their meal, they discussed the plans for tomorrow. "No way we can get them wagons down that trail, Ned," Goodnight said as he forked another steak onto his plate.

"That's for danged sure, Colonel," Ned replied. "Unless you want to drive them another thirty or forty miles down to the Tule where Colonel MacKenzie brought his wagons up when we was chasing the Cheyennes. Seems to me you're going to have to take these wagons apart, load them on the mules, and carry them down, piece by piece."

"That's a good idea, Ned, we'll plan on it," Goodnight responded.

4

As Ned and the other trail hands rolled out their blankets beneath the stars, a group of thirty Comanche braves were slipping silently out of their lodges in Indian Territory, mounting their ponies and riding unobserved off the reservation at Fort Sill.

The group, led by Buffalo Horns, a young hot-head, had decided they would not remain on the reservation where the army failed to live up to its agreement to keep them fed and clothed.

"We will return to the buffalo lands," Buffalo Horns told the other braves, "and once again kill many buffalo, dry the meat and bring it back to our families. If the White Eyes try to stop us, we will leave their bodies lying next to the bones of the buffalo that they have killed and wasted."

The other Indians grunted their approval. "I hope they try to stop us," young Wounded Bear replied, "so that we can return with their scalps."

Wounded Bear had been too young to be involved in the war with the white eyes and had never had an opportunity to count coup or take scalps.

His wish was granted sooner than he expected.

Two soldiers, stationed at nearby Fort Sill, met the group of Indians along a lonely stretch of the dusty wagon road between the Fort and the nearby village of Cache. The soldiers had been patronizing the saloons and upstairs rooms of the *painted* ladies, and were more than slightly inebriated.

"Where the hell you redskins think you're going this time of night?" one of the soldiers shouted as he weaved in his saddle.

He urged his horse up to the nearest Indian, trying to get a better look at his face in the dim light of the moon. The answer he received was a long skinning knife, plunged into his heart as Wounded Bear was granted his wish.

Before the second soldier realized what had happened, an arrow whistled through the night-time darkness and pierced his throat. Neither of the two soldiers uttered a sound as they fell from their horses. The riderless cavalry mounts bolted and headed for the Fort before the Indians were able to stop them.

Wounded Bear dismounted quickly, uttered a blood curdling scream, grabbed a handful of hair, and sliced a three inch chunk of scalp with the bloody skinning knife. He then grabbed the other soldier's hair, and quickly relieved it of a portion of its scalp. As the other warriors kicked their mounts into a run down the dusty wagon road, he vaulted onto his pony's back and followed them, holding the bloody scalps over his head while shouting his victory chant.

Riding hard throughout the night, the Indians were able to put forty miles between them and the Reservation before the sun rose in the east.

When the two riderless horses were found near the stables the next morning, guards alerted the post. The bloody saddles were witness to the fate of the riders, and General MacKenzie(promoted after the Indian wars) sent out a patrol to locate the bodies.

Four miles from the post, the bodies were found, loaded on pack mules and returned to the fort. After viewing the bodies, General MacKenzie returned to his office and began formulating plans to apprehend the recalcitrants. Corporal Kinsey, who had led the patrol which had recovered the bodies, reported that tracks indicated at least thirty unshod horses were in the group that had murdered and scalped the two cavalry privates.

"The tracks headed west away from the reservation, General," he reported as he stood at attention, next to Sergeant-Major Douglas.

"Sergeant, send a courier to Quanah's camp and tell him I want to speak to him immediately," the General ordered.

"Yes, Sir!" Sergeant-Major Timothy Douglas crisply replied, as he turned on his heels and left the General's office.

"Lieutenant Baldwin!" MacKenzie shouted through the open door.

Baldwin, who had been directing the unloading of the grisly remains of the two soldiers from the mules' backs, rushed into the office, snapped to attention and asked, "Sir?"

"Lieutenant, I want you to put together a scouting party of twelve men from your troop. Two pack animals with enough supplies for two weeks. I want those devils caught that did this and brought back to the post alive. We'll try them and hang them on the parade ground so that the rest of our charges will understand that they can't get away with murdering U.S. soldiers."

Pacing the room, he added. "If it takes more time, you

can pick up additional supplies at Fort Elliot. I don't want you returning until you have been successful in finding and capturing these murderers."

"Yes, Sir! Anything else, Sir?"

"No, Lieutenant. You know the *Llano Estacado* as well as any white man, other than Ned Armstrong and Jim Cole at the Ceebara ranch. If the trail leads anywhere near their ranch, you might enlist their aid in your search. If this is some of Quanah's braves, it'll be almost impossible to track them down."

Baldwin saluted, turned and left the room, followed by Corporal Kinsey. "Corporal, you heard the orders. Get your squad prepared. We will be leaving by noon."

Within an hour, Sergeant-Major Douglas returned with Quanah and they entered the orderly room where the General was waiting.

"Thank you, for coming, Chief," McKenzie said.

Quanah nodded. The sergeant had informed him about the murders and with the Chief's help, had searched the Comanche camp, discovering that thirty of the young warriors were missing.

"What do you know about these murders?" McKenzie asked.

Quanah, his blue eyes displaying his anger, replied. "I know nothing. My word is good--I promised to keep the peace and to keep my tribe where White Chief say we must stay. White Chief promised to keep tribe in meat and beans until we learned white man's ways. White Chief's promise was not true. Our lodges have no meat and beans. We kill our horses to feed our families and still our women and children go hungry. I, Quanah, have tried to keep the peace and have asked my people to be patient, but now some of my young warriors have refused to wait no longer. I have heard them speak of returning to the buffalo hunting grounds for meat to feed their families."

Pausing, he looked from the General to the Sergeant, then continued. "Sergeant Douglas and me, we search the camp and find empty tipis. Thirty of my young warriors are gone. Buffalo Horns, who has been trying to get me to lead the tribe back to the *Llano*, is gone. I believe he is the leader."

"I'm sending a troop after them, Chief," MacKenzie replied. "And when we find them, they will be brought back and hung for their crime."

"Is it a crime to kill for food to feed our families? Would our white brothers not kill if their families were starving?" Quanah asked.

"I understand your situation, Chief. However, we must try to solve the problem by other means which will not result in more war between our peoples. I have sent word of my anger to the Great White Father in Washington for his failure to see that food and blankets have not been sent. He has assured me that we will soon have what we need."

"But while we wait, my young warriors grow angry and impatient, and two of your soldiers lie dead. Now you are going to send more soldiers to their death, looking for Buffalo Horns and the others. They will not find them. I know Buffalo Horns--he is like the coyote. You will not find him, but he will find you. And he will fight and kill before he will be dragged back to the Fort in chains."

"That may be true, Chief, but I cannot leave your warriors to kill and murder the white buffalo hunters. They must be found and brought back."

"Then I will find them," Quanah said. "I will find them and bring them back and we will punish them for what they have done. It is my responsibility, they are my people and I gave my promise to you that my people would remain on the reservation."

MacKenzie paced the floor, his anger subsiding as he realized that Quanah was right. He had urged, even demanded, that the Indian Commission be more prompt with food and blanket shipments. The damned bureaucrats in Washington, D.C. had no sympathy for the plight of his Indian charges, and it was as Quanah had explained--there had been no shipments for three months and the Indians had only their horses to eat. *If it were me, I would probably have done the same thing as Buffalo Horns and his hot heads if I thought it would help feed my family,* he mused.

"Alright, Quanah, I will let you go after Buffalo Horns. I will give you four weeks--one moon--and if you are not back with the recalcitrants, I will come after you with all my troops and will show no mercy. How many of your warriors will you take?"

"I will take only a few of our hunters, and I will take my family--Morning Star and Jim Bold Eagle, my son. We will find Buffalo Horns and the others. We will bring them back, but we will also bring back meat and hides for our families."

"Then it is agreed. One month and I will expect you back." Turning to Sergeant Douglas, MacKenzie said, "Sergeant, inform Lieutenant Baldwin that his troop will not be leaving. You heard the agreement, we will give Quanah four weeks to locate and return with the recalcitrants. You are authorized to issue Quanah enough supplies that he feels will be needed to complete this mission."

Stepping to his desk, he took pen in hand and wrote a dispatch which he handed to the Comanche Chief. "Quanah, this paper says that I have given you permission to leave the reservation, and that you are to proceed to the *Llano Estacado* in search of Buffalo Horns and his group. No one is to interfere nor to impede your mission. Good luck."

Quanah took the folded paper and tucked it into a pocket of his buckskin jacket, turned and walked to his horse. Sergeant Douglas accompanied him to the stable where two mules were fitted with pack saddles and led to the quartermaster's supply room where they were filled with enough supplies to last twelve people a month on the prairie.

Returning to his lodge, next to the Fort, Quanah instructed Morning Star to prepare for the trip, then picked ten of his most trusted braves, mostly older men, to accompany them.

By mid-afternoon, they had found the trail left by the thirty recalcitrants and followed it to the west.

5

Colonel Goodnight had been correct, Old Blue, the big longhorn steer, had led the herd down the narrow Indian trail to the floor of the canyon. One by one the rest of the herd followed, and after four hours, the last of the eighteen hundred head reached the bottom and began to fan out, eating the lush grass along the stream's banks.

By nightfall, the wagons had been dismantled, loaded on the backs of the mules, and packed down the narrow trail. Camp was made next to the stream, and Hard Tack prepared a meal of beans and steak.

"I 'spect me and the Kid best be moving out, Colonel," Ned said, after breakfast had been completed the following morning. "My folks are going to be thinking the Indians have hung and quartered us if we don't high tail it back to Ceebara."

"I thought you was going to check out those missing mama cows over on the Canadian before you went back," Goodnight replied.

"Yes, Sir, I had a mind to, but I believe I'd best report back to Colonel Cole before I waste anymore time. If I don't, he's going to have a search party out looking for me. Besides, he's going to want to know that we got neighbors moving into the country," Ned responded.

"Alright, Ned. And I sure appreciate your help. Me and the boys would never have spotted that trail down the canyon if you hadn't pointed it out to me. You tell Colonel Cole to stop in and pay me a visit first chance he gets. We probably need to talk about boundaries. I'll be going back to get my wife, Molly, in Colorado after I get the boys settled in here. I might try to bring her back by your ranch to meet your women folks."

"I'm sure they'd be pleased, Colonel Goodnight. And you know y'all would be welcome any time," Ned said as he mounted the buckskin and headed up the trail. The Kid followed close behind, waving to their new-found friends who watched from the canyon floor.

* * * * * * *

"Yes, Sir, Colonel--a whole herd of sheep up on the Canadian. Mexicans herding them and they said there was a bunch more on up the river, from Atascosa Crossing all the way into New Mexico Territory--said they came down from Santa Fe. And a big herd of longhorns trailed in from Colorado. Belonged to a man called Goodnight, Colonel Charles Goodnight. We helped him get them down into the Palo Duro before we headed for home--said he was going back to Colorado and bring down his wife, Molly."

"What!" Jim shouted. "Sheepmen and more cowmen. Dagnab it, this place is getting plumb overcrowded. While you were gone, me and Belle found a new cow outfit just across the Canadian from our north pasture--feller named Bugbee, his wife's name is Molly, too, brought in nearly two thousand head of cows. Seemed like right nice folks, but ain't no way we're going to keep our herds separated with just a river between. And with a herd in the Palo Duro, we're going to face the same problem with cattle getting mixed."

Getting up from his chair, Jim walked out of the room onto the veranda and gazed out across the valley. Fat cows and calves had filled their bellies and were standing in the shade of the huge cottonwood trees, swishing flies with their tails. Farther across the valley, he could see a small herd of buffalo coming down the trail to water in the creek.

Ned followed him from the room and stood by his side, saying nothing until Jim spoke.

"Sheep! Cows! People! Buffalo hunters! I guess I should have expected it, Ned, but dammit, I don't like it! How we going to run our cows with all them people around. And sheep! They'll grub our grass into the ground."

"I talked to that Mexican, Romero," Ned said, "and told him we couldn't be having no sheep on our grass. I pointed out our property line and he allowed as how he'd be neighborly and keep his sheep off our grass if we'd keep our cows off of his'n."

Jim couldn't hold back a chuckle at that statement, "Well, I suppose we can live with that," he said with a grin, then added, "Goodnight, you say. Was he a big, raw-boned kind of feller--black hair and beard?

"Yes, Sir," Ned nodded in reply.

"I know him," Jim said. "He was with the rangers when they came onto that Comanche village down on the Pease back in '60. That's when they rescued Quanah's mother,

Cynthia Ann Parker. He and Jim Loving went to driving 'horns up the Colorado River to Fort Concho and then on across that dry country to the Pecos. I heard that Loving was killed by Indians somewhere over there, but I never did know what happened to Goodnight. Guess he must have taken up ranching in Colorado for a few years, if that is where he trailed that herd from."

Ned nodded his head, then said, "Colonel, me and Kid got those cows pushed back into our big lake pasture but I noticed something that's kinda got me puzzled. There must have been thirty or forty bum calves in the group. You could tell they hadn't had any milk for awhile. We searched the area pretty good and never did find their mamas, dead or alive."

"That is strange, Ned. We never have had that kind of problem before. We usually lose a few calves to coyotes and wolves, but not any cows--what you think might have happened?"

"Well, I thought maybe some buffalo hunters could have done a little target practice on them, but we didn't find any bones. Kid said maybe the hunters might have stopped hunting buffalo and started running cows--our cows--for a living. Romero didn't talk too much English, but Kid talked to him in Spanish and he said he had seen signs of some cows back north of the river. That could have been the mamas of some of those dogie calves."

"If it was, they had to have help getting across the river," Jim said. "They wouldn't just run off and leave their babies unless someone was pushing them."

"That's what I figured, Colonel. We would have gone back and searched after we helped Colonel Goodnight down into the Big Canyon, but I was afraid you folks would be getting worried about us being gone so long."

"You did right, Ned. If we do have rustler problems, no sense in rushing in and getting someone hurt. You know how mean those buffalo hunters can be. I don't want the two of you biting off more than you can chew. We'll get Slim, Sonny, Miguel and the Kid and ride up that way and look around after you've had a few days to rest up."

* * * * * * * *

Buffalo Horns and the Comanche recalcitrants followed the North Fork of the Red River out of Indian Territory and into the Texas Panhandle, knowing that they were probably being followed. They didn't, however, know that those following were members of their own tribe.

Buffalo Horns knew that once they reached the *Llano Estacado*, they would be safe. He had lived on the Plains all his life and knew every draw, every playa lake and every canyon in the area. Even if MacKenzie's cavalry was sent to get him, they would never find him.

He had one problem, however--they needed food and would have to kill the first buffalo they found. This would require time--time that he could not spare.

Then he remembered. When the tribe was recuperating at One Arm's ranch after the battle in the Big Canyon, One Arm had kept a large supply of meat--beef, buffalo and deer--hanging in a smokehouse next to the spring. Buffalo Horns, himself, had helped the ranch hands hang a dressed beef in the shed.

"We will go to One Arm's lodge," he told Wounded Bear, "and while the white eyes sleep, we will take meat from their cache, then ride onto the prairies where no one can find us."

Leaving the river bottom, the Comanches turned to the north until they could see the lights of Hidetown, then turned back west and climbed to the top of the caprock. Reaching the top, and the endless plains, they turned back north and rode along the rim of the caprock, towards Red Deer Creek.

Buffalo Horns had hunted this area many times as a boy and knew that if trouble developed he could quickly vanish in the small cedar covered canyons that he was traversing. Before dawn, the small group of Indians stopped on the brink of the caprock and looked down upon the group of moon drenched buildings which was the Ceebara ranch headquarters.

Like a wolf, Buffalo Horns sniffed the air, catching the scent of the white men, the horses, the smoke from the fires--and the aroma of curing meat in the smokehouse.

* * * * * * *

Jim, Ned, Sonny, Miguel, Billy and Slim had left the ranch headquarters at noon, the previous day, to search for signs of rustlers. Shep, the dog, had followed them out of the compound. Most of the ranch hands were at line camps several miles away, preparing to gather the cattle for marking and branding and the annual cattle drive to Dodge City.

Belle and Kate were left alone in the big house--the Garcia family, Maria and Ramon, several wives of the cowboys and a dozen children were asleep in their nearby homes. No one worried about Indians, knowing that they had all been pushed back onto the reservation.

Belle always saw to running the ranch when Jim and Ned were gone. The routine did not change--up at five a.m., breakfast, milk the three cows, feed the horses, scatter some grain for the chickens, and be ready for the heavier work schedule by the time the sun peeked over the horizon in the east.

"O.K., Cole," Kate said as she shook her ten year old son awake. "Time to get up. I need you to go to the smoke house and bring us some steaks off that yearling's hindquarter, that we butchered last week."

Cole had never been hard to awaken. He was always anxious to get out, saddle his horse and spend the day working with the other cowboys. Grandad Jim was always bragging on him, saying he was the best cowhand he had on the ranch. Besides, when he was helping with the cattle, he wasn't having to sit bored, studying his books.

He slipped on his buckskins and boots, stepped out the back door and headed for the smokehouse. He didn't need a lantern, the moon was still bright overhead--and besides, he could find his way on the darkest nights.

The ten year old was surprised to find the smokehouse door ajar when he reached to unfasten the latch. *Someone must have failed to close it properly,* he thought. *Hope there ain't no badger or skunk inside.*

Stepping into the darkened room, he reached for the hanging hindquarter of beef and began slicing off a sizable chunk, when someone grabbed his wrist, held it tightly while another hand covered his mouth. His cry of surprise was stifled by the hand over his mouth.

Pulling hard, he was able to free his knife hand and slashed at his unseen adversary. He felt the knife go deep in his attacker's leg as he struggled to free himself. Then the world went black as something smashed him against the ear. His small body went limp and strong hands carried him from the building.

Buffalo Horns carried the small boy to the tethered horses outside the compound, while the other Comanches cut down several chunks of the hanging meat and rushed to join him at the horses. No one in the nearby houses were aware of the Indians' presence.

Young Cole was lifted onto Buffalo Horns horse, and the Comanche mounted behind him. Quietly, the thirty mounted horsemen rode away from the ranch.

* * * * * * * *

"Where is that boy?" Kate asked as she looked out into the darkened yard. "He beats all. I sent him after meat thirty minutes ago--I bet he found a possum or coon and forgot all about what I sent him to do," she told her mother.

The two women were busy starting fires in the cook stove, rolling out biscuit dough and preparing for breakfast, unaware that the ten year old was being carried quietly away by the marauding Indians.

After nearly an hour, Kate said, "I guess I'm going to have to go get that beef myself if we're going to have any for breakfast. I'll swear, but I can't depend on him to do anything I tell him. All he's got on his mind is chasing wild animals and riding that horse."

Dawn was beginning to break as she stepped out the door and headed for the smokehouse. Belle heard her scream and rushed outside to see what had happened. She found Kate standing in the middle of the smokehouse, looking at the meat on the floor, and the empty hooks hanging above. She could see several moccasin prints in the sandy soil leading away from the smoke house.

"Oh, my Lord!" she cried, "Indians!"

The two women rushed back to the house and grabbed two Winchesters from the gun rack then returned to the smokehouse and followed the moccasin tracks out of the compound. A hundred yards outside the gate, they found where the Indian ponies had been tethered and could see the trail leading away towards the caprock.

"Do you think they've got Cole?" Kate asked her mother.

"I don't see his tracks anywhere," Belle replied. "He came into the smokehouse but there are no tracks leaving. They must have carried him out and put him on one of the horses."

Kate began to cry. "What will we do?" she asked.

Belle, hurting deeply inside, realizing that her grandson was being abducted by Indians, refused to show panic. She placed her arms around Kate and held her close. "We'll find him, don't you worry," she said.

6

Quanah followed the tracks of the recalcitrants up the Red River, west of Hidetown, then north to the Ceebara compound. His heart skipped when he realized that Buffalo Horns was headed directly for the ranch house--afraid of what he might find if the hot-heads had caught the folks at the ranch unawares.

As they rode up, he was surprised to be greeted by the ladies of the ranch, Winchesters glistening in the sun and pointed directly at his group. He stopped two hundred yards from the gate, held up his hand in peace, thinking that they would be welcome.

However, a shot kicked up dust at his horse's feet--he quickly wheeled his horse around, motioned for the others to do the same, and ducked into the cover of the cottonwood grove.

Tying a white rag onto the barrel of his rifle, he slowly emerged from the grove and rode towards Belle and Kate. Belle held her fire until she recognized that it was Quanah.

"It is me, Quanah," he shouted. "I come in peace."

"Where is my son?" Kate shouted. "Bring me Cole."

"I do not have Cole," Quanah answered. "If he is missing, then Buffalo Horns, who I follow, has him. I wish to talk."

The women did not lower their rifles, but motioned for Quanah to approach.

Quanah stopped the tall chestnut stallion, the one which had been a gift from One Arm, ten paces in front of Kate and spoke. "Buffalo Horns and many of my braves killed two soldiers at the white man's fort, then ran for the buffalo grounds. White Chief, MacKenzie, asked me to bring them back. He gave paper," reaching into his jacket, he pulled the dispatch out and handed it to Kate.

Reluctantly, she stepped forward and took the paper, examined it and returned it. Turning to Kate, she said, "He's telling the truth. It was not his group that took Cole."

Quanah turned and motioned to Morning Star and the others to come forward. When Kate saw the young Indian woman, she rushed forward to meet her, for they had been friends for many years. When Jim Bold Eagle had been only a few days old, Quanah had brought Morning Star and her papoose to visit his friends at the ranch--and when the Colonel had been wounded by the buffalo hunters, and Belle had been raped by the grisly group, Quanah and his braves had killed the hunters and rescued his friends. He carried them back to his village and Morning Star had nursed Jim back to health, saving his life.

Kate led the group into the compound and Quanah instructed the men to wait in the shade of the huge cottonwood as he, Morning Star and Jim Bold Eagle accompanied the two women into the ranch house.

Quickly, Belle told Quanah what had happened--that young Cole was missing and all of the men of the ranch were gone. She and Kate were preparing to follow the tracks of the Indian raiders, knowing that they were placing their lives, as well as that of her grandson, in danger.

"You no go," Quanah said. "I will find Cole. He Bold Eagle's friend. I will bring him back."

The two boys were the same age. Young Cole Armstrong had been born only weeks after Quanah's son, Jim Bold Eagle had been born. Quanah had named his son after his friend, One Arm. Both boys had played together many times, racing their ponies at breakneck speed up and down the valley, enjoying each other's company, and Cole had spent many nights in Quanah's tipi--as had Jim Bold Eagle spent nights in Cole's bed.

"Thank you, Quanah," Kate replied, but I must go with you. "My son is in danger and I must do all within my power to help him."

While Belle packed food and clothing, Kate rushed to the corral, caught their horses, saddled them and led them to the hitching post in front of the ranch house.

* * * * * * * *

The Colonel, Ned and the other cowboys made early camp on the Canadian at the old site of Adobe Walls. The buffalo hunters camp had been burned by the Indians after the hunters had abandoned it in '74, and grass had grown up around the ruins.

As they prepared beans and bacon over a small campfire, made from the burned out remains of the buildings, the sound of a Sharp's fifty caliber rifle could be heard in the distance. Fifteen shots were fired over a period of fifteen minutes. As the sound of the shots echoed through the canyons along the river bed, Jim said, "That's fifteen more buffalo that won't be roaming these plains anymore if that hunter can shoot worth a durned. But the coyotes and buzzards will have a feast after the skinners get their hides. Such a waste!"

"Yes, Sir, Colonel," Ned replied, then pointed at a pile of white bones glistening in the evening sun which lay no more than three hundred yards north of their campground, the remains of thirty buffalo which had been killed the previous year. "Ain't going to be long before there's nothing left of the shaggy herds 'ceptin those piles of dry bones to remind us that this was once buffalo and Indian country."

The coffee water had started boiling over the fire and Ned reached for the pot and poured them two cups. Handing one to Jim, he stared thoughtfully into the steaming cup, then said, "Colonel, how come buffalo hunters were ever allowed to come into this area and start killing all the buffalo? I thought this land was given to the Indians in a treaty."

"It was, Ned. The Medicine Lodge Treaty was signed in '67 which gave the Indians all of the land south of the Arkansas River as their hunting grounds, ' *for as long as the grass grows and the buffalo roam*'. But when the demand for hides in Europe became so great, the price of prime hides went up to five or six dollars. It didn't take long for hunters to kill most of the shaggies north of the Arkansas. Then they started pressuring the government to allow them to hunt south of the river. General Sherman recognized that the buffalo was the Indians' commissary, and in order for him to keep the tribes on the reservation, the buffalo herds, their commissary, would have to be destroyed. He looked the other way, when the hunters started moving into treaty lands. Of course, when the Indians went on the warpath and started killing the white hunters for invading their lands, it gave him an excuse to bring in the cavalry to protect U.S. citizens. So killing the buffalo was actually a government policy to rid the plains of the Indian tribes."

Shaking his head in disgust, Jim added, "They call that progress, Ned; white man's progress! Since the Indians have been pushed onto the reservation, the next thing that's going to happen to this land is nesters are going to come in and start plowing up the grass for crops, and there won't even be enough grazing left for our cattle. An old Indian once told me that *'what white man can't plow up, he shit on,"* -- and damned if I don't believe he was right."

Ned smiled, nodding his head in agreement. "What we going to do when the nester's show up, Colonel? They going to take our land?"

"Not without a fight, Ned. It may be a legal battle that we'll have to fight in Austin, but we have our land grant papers from the legislature, setting out our property lines. But that was made when Texas was still a Republic--now that it's a state, land grabbers may try to say it ain't legal."

As they sat talking and drinking their coffee, Sonny and the Kid rode in after scouting upriver a few miles, where they were looking for signs of cattle north of the Canadian.

"Colonel, we didn't find any tracks at all. If there ever was any, that rain two nights ago washed away any signs," Sonny said, as he dismounted, stretched and reached for the coffee pot.

Kid took the reins of Sonny's horse and led the two mounts to where the other horses were tethered, unsaddled them and returned to the fire.

"We probably ain't far enough west, Colonel," he said as he poured himself a cup of the boiling coffee. "That buffalo camp at Atascosa Crossing is still a day's ride upriver, and that's where Romero said he saw signs of cattle north of the river."

"I 'spect you're right, Billy. But there's lots of canyons between here and there. No use in being in too big a hurry. Everything is alright at the ranch with the Indians shoved back on the reservation. We'll just keep looking, never can tell what we might turn up."

* * * * * * *

Buffalo Horns and his group of Comanches rode hard after leaving the ranch headquarters. Cole had regained consciousness and had been placed on a spare pony which the Indians had brought. By mid-afternoon, they were on top of the *Llano*, ten miles south of the Adobe Walls ruins.

Unknown to Buffalo Horns, Quanah, Belle, Kate, Morning Star, Jim Bold Eagle and the other members of Quanah's tribe were in hot pursuit, following the well marked trail left by the thirty recalcitrants.

Buffalo Horns saw several small herds of buffalo as they traveled to the west and would have liked to stop and make his hunt here, but he realized that he needed to put as much distance between himself and the ranch as possible. They surely had missed the boy by now and would be trying to find his trail. He hadn't decided what to do with Cole--maybe he would kill him and leave him for the coyotes--but he was a strong boy, maybe he could sell him to Comanchero traders. He knew there were usually traders in the canyon, called

Ransom, to the south. Maybe they would go there after they had killed many buffalo.

Approaching a small playa with an ample supply of water from the rain two days before, Buffalo Horns called a halt. "We camp here, our horses need rest. Tomorrow we will make our hunt."

The smoked meat which they had stolen from the white-eyes filled their bellies and they were soon asleep, exhausted from the long ride from the fort. However, as the sun slipped slowly towards the horizon in the west, their rest was interrupted by the sound of gunfire just over the ridge to the north.

Buffalo Horns rushed to his horse, thinking that they were being attacked, but soon realized that the shots were coming from one of the big guns he had heard the white eyes use to kill the buffalo.

He counted, as the gun slowly fired in the distance. Finally, it stopped after he counted fifteen. Fifteen buffalo were probably lying dead in the grass, he reasoned.

"Let us go and kill the white eyes," Wounded Bear said as he listened to the last shot being fired. "We can get their scalps and take their buffalo."

"We will wait," Buffalo Horns replied. "The big guns that kill the buffalo will also kill the Comanche. When darkness comes and the hunters are resting, we will attack."

Wounded Bear did not like to wait, he had come for scalps and was anxious to kill, as were the other young warriors.

* * * * * * *

Quanah heard the sound of the big Sharps rifle as he loped his horse, following the trail of Buffalo Horns and his other tribesmen. The sound was coming from a great distance, probably five or six miles ahead.

Kate and Belle were close behind, but the others had fallen back a couple hundred yards, unable to keep up with the long-legged chestnut stallion.

Quanah counted--thirteen, fourteen, fifteen. The shots ended. He remembered the sound and vision of bloated, naked bodies of slaughtered buffalo flashed across his mind-- bodies that he had seen the last day he rode across the prairies with his friend, One Arm. That was the day he agreed to go to the white man's reservation to make a new life for his people. The thought brought forth a feeling of anger.

Belle and Kate also heard the shots, and at first believed that the Indians were probably killing young Cole. However, when the shots continued, they realized that somewhere ahead, a party of buffalo hunters were making a kill.

Quanah stopped and waited for the others to catch up. "We must go carefully," he said. "Buffalo Horns will have heard the big gun and will be watching. We must not allow him to see us before we are able to free the boy."

They rode on more slowly, watching over each rise to make certain they did not ride into Buffalo Horns' camp.

Meanwhile, Buffalo Horns and his warriors were crawling silently through the grass, having staked their ponies in a dry arroyo a mile from the hunters camp. The sun had reached the horizon as the buffalo hunters removed the last hide from the fifteen downed shaggies, rolled it and threw it onto one of the wagons.

There were five men in the group, a large man who appeared to be the leader, who was leaning against a wagon wheel with the butt of his rifle resting on the ground.

One of the skinners had already started a fire of buffalo chips and was roasting buffalo steaks over the fire. Another was filling the dirty coffee pot with water from the barrel lashed to the side of one of the wagons. Pouring in a handful of ground coffee, he placed the pot on a bed of the glowing coals.

The other hunters threw their bedrolls around the fire and sat down, waiting for the steaks to cook.

"Damned shame there weren't more shaggies in that bunch," the dirty hunter said as he sipped the fresh brewed coffee. "Fifteen head and I killed 'em all. Looks like these herds get smaller every day. I been thinking we'll take these hides back to Hidetown, then head on south. Probably be a lot more buffaler down that way, where there won't be so many hunters taking them."

As he reached for the pot to refill his tin cup, he heard a quiet swish of air, then felt the arrow go deep in his chest. As he fell forward into the fire, the last thing he saw, before death closed his mind, was the shafts of arrows protruding from the backs and chests of the other members of his hunting party. The air was filled with the piercing victory cry of the Comanche warriors as they rose from the tall grass and rushed forward to take their battle trophies.

Quick work was made of removing the scalps from the dead hunters. The bloody bodies were dragged away from the fire and the Indians calmly sat on the hunters blankets and began eating the steaks which the hunters had prepared.

Young Cole was brought forward from the darkness by one of the younger warriors who had been given the job of watching him and keeping him quiet while the raid was made. Buffalo Horns threw him a charred piece of meat, which he began to chew hungrily.

Another warrior appeared out of the darkness, leading the Indians' ponies, and began tieing them to the wagons.

With their bellies full, the Indians sat around the small fire and bragged about their bravery and accuracy with their arrows. Those who had not been first on the scene and had taken no scalps, began collecting other trophies from the bodies of the dead hunters--skinning knives, pistols, gun belts and tobacco.

Soon, the excitement of the battle waned, and one after the other curled up on blankets and fell asleep. Buffalo Horns threw Cole a dirty blanket. Then he was tied to the back of the hide wagon, and the young boy fell asleep, wondering what the Indians had planned for him tomorrow.

7

Quanah, Belle, Kate and the others led their horses slowly and cautiously through the night, following the moonlit trail in the grass. About midnight, they came upon the original camp of the recalcitrants next to the small playa lake.

Quanah felt of the remains of the buffalo chip fire and discovered it was still warm, then followed the dim trail which led away from the lakeshore to the north. Pausing, he motioned for Belle to come forward.

"Buffalo Horns heard the big guns and has gone to attack the hunter's camp. It must be nearby. I will take my men and we will find them," he said.

"No," Belle said. "Kate and I will go with you. I must help to save my grandson."

Although Quanah did not like it, he did not argue and agreed that they all would go. He knew there were thirty warriors in the group of recalcitrants and perhaps these two women with their Winchesters would be of help if he were forced to fight them.

After they had walked only a short distance, Quanah's keen nose picked up the scent of stinking buffalo hides and knew that the buffalo hunters camp was just over the next small rise. Leaving the others behind, he, Belle and Kate slipped silently forward. Reaching the top of the small knoll, they looked over into a small depression on the prairie floor and saw the wagons. Coals from the campfire still glowed in the dark, and Quanah's keen eyesight began to pick out the forms around the wagon. He could tell that it was Indians asleep around the campfire, but where were the buffalo hunters?

Then his eyes picked out the form of several bodies piled a short distance away from the wagons--bodies of the dead hunters.

He was too late. Buffalo Horns had already attacked and killed--more blood on his hands, more reason that he would be hung when Quanah took him back to the fort.

Letting his eyes roam around the camp, Quanah soon picked out the small form of Cole lying at the rear of the hide wagon. The nearest Comanche was asleep twenty feet away. Motioning to Belle, they retreated back to the group waiting a hundred yards behind.

Reaching the others, Kate said, "I am going to slip in and release my son, Quanah."

"No!" Quanah replied, emphatically. "Any noise and Buffalo Horns would hear you. There is no place for you to hide, even in the dark. The grass is deep, and my son Jim Bold Eagle is small. I have taught him to crawl like the snake, he can reach the camp without being seen, even if Buffalo Horns is awake. The grass will hide him."

Kneeling before his son, Quanah placed his hands on the boy's shoulders and said, "It is time for you to become a warrior. You must go quietly my son. Do not rush. You must be like the snake and stay close to the ground."

Reaching to his belt, he pulled his long skinning knife from its scabbard and handed it to the boy. "You must slip quietly to your friend at the wagon and cut the ropes that hold him, then lead him back to us. When you awaken him, place your hand over his mouth so that he makes no sound. Do you understand?"

"Yes, Father," the Indian boy replied, proudly. He knew that Quanah was placing a great responsibility on his shoulders and he would not fail. This was his friend, Cole Armstrong, who was being held, and he would do as his father commanded.

Dropping to the ground and lying flat on his stomach he began to crawl slowly towards the camp. The grass was tall and hid his small body from view. Stopping, he slowly lifted his head above the grass to get his bearing and could see that he was about fifty yards from the camp but there was a sleeping warrior between him and Cole.

Slowly, he changed direction and crawled a short distance before once again stopping and looking. Now there was no one between him and Cole and he continued to crawl in the direction of his young friend.

Reaching the sleeping boy, he placed his hand over Cole's mouth and whispered in his ear. "It is I, Jim Bold Eagle, do not make a sound. I will cut your ropes and you must follow me quietly. We must crawl as we used to do when we would hunt the deer. My father and your mother wait for us over the hill."

Cole could hardly believe his ears, but he recognized his

young friend in the moonlight, and followed close behind as Jim Bold Eagle crawled slowly and quietly back to the spot where Quanah waited.

Kate took him in her arms and squeezed, without saying a word but letting him know that he was now safe. They moved quietly back to the shore of the small playa.

"We will wait until morning and I will talk to Buffalo Horns and tell him that he must accompany me back to the fort," Quanah said.

Belle nodded in agreement, but asked, "And if Buffalo Horns refuses, he has thirty guns to keep you from taking him. What will we do then?"

"I will have my warriors around their camp, and if they refuse, then we will fight."

"Then we will help," Kate said. "You have saved my son, now we must repay you."

Quanah realized it would do no good to argue with these female white eyes. He could tell his women what to do and they would obey, but not these two red haired women.

"It is so," he said, disgustedly. "If you are to fight, then we all fight, Morning Star and my son." With that he gave each of them a rifle, including Cole--and instructed them to be very careful.

As the sun began to rise in the east and the prairie became ablaze with its rays, Quanah arose from the grass and stood majestically on the lip of the hill, a hundred yards from the buffalo hunters camp where Buffalo Horns and the other Comanches lay sleeping--his Winchester resting loosely in his right hand.

"Buffalo Horns!" he shouted. "It is I, Quanah!"

The leader of the recalcitrants jumped quickly to his feet, grabbing his rifle and pointing it in the direction of Quanah. Pumping a shell into the chamber, he fired quickly without taking aim and the bullet kicked up dirt and grass at Quanah's feet.

Quanah quickly fell to the ground, and the grass hid him from view of Buffalo Horns. The other Indians quickly grabbed their rifles and sought shelter behind the wagons.

"Buffalo Horns!" Quanah again shouted. "I have come to take you back to the fort. You have broken my promise to MacKenzie that we would travel the white man's ways. Now we must go back and make it right."

"I will never go back," Buffalo Horns replied, "We have killed soldiers and now we have taken the scalps of hunters who are killing our buffalo. The white chief would hang me and all of my warriors. We will remain in the land of the buffalo."

With that, he pointed his rifle at the spot where he had seen Quanah fall, and fired again.

* * * * * * * *

Colonel Cole, Ned, Sonny, Miguel and Billy had broken camp and were mounting their horses when they heard the shots.

"That's a Winchester, Colonel," Ned said as he looked in the direction of the sound. "Buffalo hunters don't shoot buffalo with Winchesters."

"I think you're right, Ned. Maybe we'd better take a look. Might be someone in trouble."

They splashed their horses across the sandy river bed, the water rising to the horses' knees. Reaching the other side of the stream, they kicked the horses into a gallop, riding in the direction of the sound as more shots were heard.

Buffalo Horns and the other recalcitrants began a steady fire in the direction where Quanah had disappeared. Quanah held his fire, and instructed the others to keep down and wait for his command. He intended to try one last time to reason with Buffalo Horns, but he never had the chance.

Buffalo Horns motioned to his men under the wagon to follow him, and he arose and began running towards Quanah's position. The others followed him, laying down a withering fire into the grass where Quanah and his group were hidden.

Quanah gave the order to fire, and fourteen guns spoke as one. Three of the attacking recalcitrants fell, the others continued to run forward.

Morning Star, fearing for Quanah's life, rose with her rifle pointed towards Buffalo Horns. Buffalo Horns fired, and Morning Star was knocked backwards by the force of the bullet, blood coloring her buckskins red.

Buffalo Horns continued to rush the hidden shooters, and when it appeared that they would overrun Quanah's position, five mounted horsemen appeared charging from the right, guns blazing. Jim, Ned, Sonny, Miguel and Billy rushed into the battle and Buffalo Horns' warriors panicked, turned and rushed back towards the wagons.

They were too late, however, as Jim and his group pulled their horses up next to the wagons, trapping Buffalo Horns between them and Quanah's group.

"Put down your guns," Quanah shouted, "It is over!"

The twenty-five warriors who remained standing dropped their rifles--Buffalo Horns held his rifle high in defiance.

"I will kill you, Buffalo Horns," Quanah shouted as he arose from the grass, "if you do not do as I say."

Without hesitating, Buffalo Horns turned his rifle back towards Quanah, but before he could pull the trigger, Ned, who had his rifle sighted on a spot between the huge Indian's shoulder, fired. As Buffalo Horn's fell forward, his finger tightened on the trigger, but the shot only kicked up dirt and grass ten yards in front of Quanah.

Looking around to see if any of his group was hurt, Quanah spotted Morning Star, lying face up, with her life blood slowly coloring the grass.

Screaming, he rushed to her side, knelt and placed her head in his lap. She feebly lifted her hand, touched his lips and smiled, then closed her eyes in death.

Quanah held her to his breast, rocking forward and back, and began to chant the death song of the Comanche. Young Jim Bold Eagle rushed forward, fell to the ground and took his mother's limp hand in his own, and joined his father's death chant.

The group of cowboys and Indians gathered around them, and silently watched as tears flowed down their cheeks.

Of the three other Indians who were shot, only one was dead, Wounded Bear, the young warrior who wished to have many scalps hanging from his belt. The other two were not seriously injured and were able to ride.

Buffalo Horn's dead warriors were buried where they

died, but Quanah requested that Morning Star be carried back to the ranch house and buried in the cottonwood grove where he would always be able to visit her when he visited his friends.

Jim Bold Eagle, Quanah's ten year old son, had received a flesh wound in his arm, a wound of which he was very proud. Now he would be looked upon as a brave warrior by his friends. It was difficult for him not to cry because of the loss of his mother, but Comanche warriors don't cry.

Belle and Kate fussed over him, cleaning the wound and wrapping it with a clean cloth--and thanked him for rescuing Cole.

"We will all return to the Ceebara ranch house," Jim told Quanah. "We will bury my friend and your wife, Morning Star, where we can watch over the grave. You will have plenty of time to take buffalo from the herd along the Red Deer Creek before returning to the fort, and we can help you with the skinning and curing of the meat."

Quanah thanked him, and, taking the recalcitrants aside, talked to them sternly. "You have done wrong. Comanche's word is good but you have broken our promise to remain on the white man's reservation in peace. For that you must be punished. But I will speak to the white chief, MacKenzie, and tell him that you were only trying to find food for our people. MacKenzie is fair--his words are straight. Maybe he will allow Comanches to pass judgement for breaking our word."

The young men looked cowed as their chief berated them, and Quanah could see that they understood they had brought shame on the tribe. "I do not wish to take you back like whipped dogs. I will not tie you but I tell you, if you try to run away, I will track you down and I will leave you to die, staked to an ant bed," he said.

The young warriors nodded in agreement.

* * * * * * * *

The hunt was a good one. Quanah, convinced that the warriors who had bolted the reservation, would give no problems, allowed them to participate in the hunt with their bows and arrows.

The buffalo were found grazing between the Red Deer Creek and the Washita River, below but in sight of the caprock, a distance of only ten miles from the ranch headquarters. This herd of approximately three thousand head had been protected from the guns of the buffalo hunters by Colonel Cole and the cowboys of Ceebara.

Quanah thrilled at the sight of the huge herd, realizing that he was going to be able to make one last hunt of the shaggy animals. He led the hunters down a deep arroyo which would take them within two hundred yards of the animals before they would be seen.

Bursting out of the arroyo, they were in the midst of the herd before the shaggies realized that they were being invaded. Sharp arrows penetrated the heart of three of the animals before they began running from the shouting warriors. Riding alongside of the running buffalo, the young men let fly their arrows and animal after animal fell as the sharp projectiles found vital organs.

The Indians were elated, running their horses and shouting their hunting cry. Colonel Cole, Ned and the other cowboys sat their horses on a ridge and watched, as the Indians took their pleasure.

Ned had brought his big Sharps and had dismounted, lying in the grass, ready to fire if it looked as if the Indians were not going to be able to kill enough of the herd. It was apparent that he was not needed as the prairie floor became littered with dying buffalo.

Suddenly, a huge bull with an arrow dangling from his neck, turned on Quanah's horse, and with head lowered, charged. Before Quanah could turn his pony away, the bull struck its left foreleg, upsetting horse and rider.

Losing his bow, Quanah quickly regained his feet but his horse had already bolted and had rejoined the other horses as their riders pursued the stampeding herd.

Quanah stood helpless as the wounded bull turned and charged the horse less Indian.

Ned, realizing Quanah's dilemma, quickly pulled the sights of the big Sharps around, locked in on the bulls shoulder, and squeezed the trigger. The shot echoed down the valley as the bull fell to his knees within two feet of the helpless Indian. Quanah reached out his arms and placed his hands on the bulls horns in an effort to protect himself--as the buffalo fell over, blood gushing from the huge hole made by the fifty caliber slug.

As the stampeding herd rushed towards Quanah, Jim spurred the big black stallion across the prairie to the Indian's aid. As he pulled up beside the downed bull, he motioned and Quanah grabbed his hand and leaped upward, landing on the stallions hips behind the saddle. Within seconds, the stallion had carried his two riders to safety.

Ned watched as the herd disappeared over the ridge and the Comanches returned to the scene of their slaughter. Thirty buffalo lay dying, proof of their accuracy with bows and arrows.

As the Comanches went about the task of skinning and dressing out the shaggies, two Ceebara wagons appeared on the scene, and the meat was loaded by the cowboys. However, the two wagons would not carry all of the dressed out meat, and the Indians were forced to carry some on their ponies.

By nightfall, the hunting party had returned to ranch headquarters and the job of slicing and smoking the meat into jerky began. For three days, fires burned day and night in the cottonwood grove, as the meat was cured and wrapped in hides, to be hauled back to their families on the Reservation.

"I have spare wagons," Jim told his friend, Quanah. "Take what you need to carry the meat and hides back to your people. I did not know that the government had failed to send the agreed upon rations to your people, and am saddened that your people have faced hunger. I wish to give you a herd of cattle, so that you may raise your own beef and your people will not be hungry again. Had it not been for the friendship of your tribe, we would never have been able to build our herds. Now I wish to repay you. My cowboys will bring them to you, soon; when they return, they can bring the wagons."

"One Arm is good friend," Quanah replied, "my people thank you."

"I have a request of you, my friend," Jim said. "Let Jim Bold Eagle remain with me for awhile. I will teach him the ways of the cow. He can learn with my grandson, Cole. We will teach him to read and write the white man's language so he will grow to be a great Chief for your people."

Quanah realized that this would be good for his son, now that his mother was dead. He was now ten years old, going on eleven and needed to learn the white man's ways. The old life was now gone--there would be no more roaming the prairies and chasing the buffalo for his people. They had grass, good grass on the reservation, and they needed their own longhorns so that they would not have to depend on the Great Chief in Washington to feed and cloth them.

Nodding his head sadly, Quanah said, "Yes, I will leave my son with you, as I leave my beautiful Morning Star. I know you will care for him and teach him many things which he cannot learn at the fort."

Holding up his hands, he showed all ten fingers, "I will leave him for this many moons and we will see what he learns."

8

September arrived and the cattle were brought down from the *Llano*, herded into pens below the ranch house, and the new calf crop was cut out for marking and branding.

As Jim suspected, when the cattle from the Canadian River pasture, north of the headquarters, were brought in, there were more than a hundred head of cows bearing the Quarter Circle T brand mixed with the C Bar A cattle. "Cut 'em out and head 'em back north," he instructed Sonny and the Kid. "Maybe they'll find their way back to the Bugbee's without our help. We'll check it out later, and push them back across the river." Then, to no one in particular, he added, disgustedly, "Neighbors within thirty miles of the ranch house--what else could you expect!"

Young Cole and Jim Bold Eagle, riding their ponies, helped in the roundup. They had become almost as proficient as the best of the cowhands, keeping the stragglers from cutting back away from the herd. Jim watched them with deep satisfaction, marveling at their ability as horsemen. *Guess they should be,* he thought, *they've been riding horses longer than they've been walking.*

After the cattle were penned, the branding and castrating of the calves began. Slim and three of his best ropers would cut out a calf, throw their loops under the calves belly and snag its two hind feet and drag it to the branding fire where the branding crew held red-hot branding irons, ready to burn the C Bar A brand on the left hip. Sharp knives were used to relieve the bull calves of their testicals, changing them from bulls to steers. When the ropes were released from the calves, the two boys drove them into an adjoining pen, where they were held overnight to make certain that the bleeding from the castration had stopped.

This work was completed in two weeks and the older bulls, mamas and babies were driven to the Washita pasture. The three year old steers were cut back and made ready for the trail drive to the railroad at Dodge City.

Sitting on the veranda of the ranch house, sipping coffee and munching on Maria's cookies, the Colonel and Ned were discussing plans for the cattle drive to Dodge City. "Colonel, seems to me we're missing some cattle. There should be more three-year old steers, and there was way too many dogie calves in the cut."

"That's the way I see it, too, Ned," Jim replied. "Some of the older cows didn't show up in the *gather*. Remember that big old blue roan cow that got one horn broke off last year when she tried to run through the corral? I never could find her in the bunch, and she would have been easy to spot. And that old pinto cow that has had three sets of twins in the last five years--she's missing, also."

Even with twenty-five thousand head of cattle, a good cattleman could remember almost everyone on sight--and especially if they showed up missing.

"Guess we should have gone back and looked across the river at Atascosa crossing after we had that run-in with Quanah's braves. Even though the rains had washed out any signs, we might have found some strays--if they were strays," Ned said.

"If they were strays, they'll still be out there somewhere. Rough as those canyons are on the north side of the river, they'll be able to make the winter fine. Maybe we'll find them next spring," Jim said as he set his coffee cup down and pulled out one of his long, black cigars, clamped it between his teeth, struck a match and lit it. He blew a plume of smoke before continuing.

"I 'spect we won't find them, though--unless we look in the packing houses in Chicago. If rustlers took 'em, they probably went straight to Dodge City with them and got mixed with all them other Texas 'horns coming up the Chisholm Trail. They are probably steak and gravy by now," he said.

"You're probably right, Colonel," Ned answered, "but I'm going to do some scouting around when we get the herd into Dodge. Every buyer there knows our C Bar A brand. If someone brought a herd in carrying our brand, they'll remember."

"Can't hurt anything to look, but I'm betting that if rustlers took 'em, they won't be carrying our brand any more," Jim reflected.

Picking up another cookie and taking a bite, Ned asked. "What do you mean, once that C Bar A is burned into their hide, they ain't going to be able to make it disappear."

"No, but a running iron sure might make it appear different. I never saw a brand yet that some smart drifter couldn't change by running a hot iron over it. A couple of months of new hair growing around it could make it look like it was original."

Ned nodded his head in understanding. "Guess we're going to have to catch 'em in the act, Colonel," he said.

* * * * * * * *

"Pa," Cole said as he and Bold Eagle were pulling the saddles from their horses after helping push the cows and calves into the Washita pasture, "I wish I could help make this drive to Dodge City. I'm ten years old and ain't never been to Dodge. Ma never would let me go before because she said I was too young and there was too much Indian danger. Well, I'm not young anymore and there ain't any Indians to worry about, and I can herd cows as well as any of your hands. I sure wish you'd let me go."

Ned, with his back to Cole, smiled at the argument his son was making. *Not young anymore,* he thought. *Ten years old and he thinks he's grown-up already Well, I'll say one thing, he's right about herding cows as good as any of the cowhands. The boy is a natural cowboy.*

"I could certainly use the help, Son. I know you and Bold Eagle would carry your load fine. And Quanah wanted Bold Eagle to learn all he could about running cows--he could learn a lot on a cattle drive. But you know your Ma. She's bound and determined that your shirttail is still too short." Pausing, and as if in deep thought, he finally added. "But I tell you what--you convince her that you're old enough and I'll let you go along."

"Yippee!!" Cole yelled, as he ran for the ranch house. Bursting into the kitchen, breathless, he shouted, "Ma, Pa says I can go on the drive to Dodge City with him, long as it's alright with you!"

"Well, you just calm down, young man--it's not alright with me. You're still just a baby and haven't got any business making a long drive like that. Besides, Dodge City is nothing but a sin hole, and I don't want you seeing what goes on in a place like that."

"Please, Ma!" Cole begged. "I already know everything that goes on in Dodge City. All the hands have told me about them pretty saloon ladies and how the buffalo hunters fight for their attention. I ain't going to see anything that I don't already know. Besides, Grandpa says I'm as good a cowhand as any of the other cowboys, and Pa says he could use the help. Please!"

"I said no, Cole, and that's the end of it. Your shirttail ain't long enough yet. Maybe next year," Kate said as she shoved a pan of biscuits into the oven.

There it is again, my shirttail ain't long enough--every time I want to do something grown-up, they say my shirt - tail ain't long enough. Well, I'll show them!

Cole had been taught not to argue. Once his mother had set her foot down, he knew to keep his mouth shut. He went outside and washed his face and hands in the wash pan by the kitchen door, then sat down on the stump by the wood pile and pouted, until Kate announced that supper was ready. Bold Eagle, never one to say much, was already at the table when Cole sat down.

Cole had nothing to say during the meal, but listened as Ned and the Colonel discussed plans for the beginning of the drive tomorrow.

"I think we're ready, Colonel," Ned said. "I'm taking along an empty wagon to bring back a load of supplies, and the chuck wagon is loaded with enough beans, bacon, flour, sugar and salt to make the drive. We'll butcher a steer on the way for beef."

Jim nodded in agreement. He was pleased that Ned had learned the business so well. No longer did he have to do all the planning. Ned had taken over much of the responsibility, leaving him more time to share with his lovely Belle.

"What you think the herd will be worth this year," he asked.

"It don't look too, good, Colonel. Billy Dixon was telling me that they've closed down the pens at Abilene and Ellsworth because of the fever, and all the herds coming up the Chisholm Trail are now coming into Dodge. With that many herds, the buyers may be a little hard to deal with. I 'spect we'll be looking at a weak market."

"Well, just remember Ned, our herd will be fat and slick when they get there with just ten days on the trail. Those other herds are going to be lean as a rail after being on the trail for two months. Ceebara cattle should bring top money," Jim said.

Without a word, Cole slipped from the table and went to his room. Bold Eagle followed.

"What's eating the boy," Jim asked, "he hardly touched his food?"

Kate spoke up, "He's pouting because I won't agree to let

him go with his Pa tomorrow."

"Well, Kate," Jim said, "the boy is a hard worker, and rides that horse as good as any of our cowboys. It might be time to let him start growing up."

"He's just ten years old, Colonel. He's got plenty of time to start growing up. Maybe next year," Kate said as she started gathering the dishes from the table.

The coal oil lamp burned late in Cole's room that night, and now and then the two boys were heard laughing.

The next morning, after the chores were done and Kate announced that breakfast was ready, the two boys marched in and stood in the middle of the room, smiling like a possum in a gum tree.

They were still standing when the Colonel and Ned sat down and Belle brought in a steaming pan of biscuits. "Set down, boys," Kate said, as she began pouring coffee.

"We got something to show you, first," Cole said. "You said our shirttails was too short to make the cattle drive. We just want to show you that you're wrong."

Turning around, they pulled their shirttails from inside their pants and the tails fell below their knees. During the night, they had sewn another foot of cloth onto the tails of their shirts!

Jim and Ned laughed their approval at the boys quick thinking. Kate frowned, but had to turn her head to keep the boys from seeing the smile that was forming at the corners of her mouth.

"They've got you there, Kate," the Colonel said, "looks to me like you couldn't ask for longer shirtttails than that."

Ned, laughing, added his support for the boys. "Kate, any

body as quick-witted as that ought to be allowed to make their first cattle drive. I'll see to it that they aren't hurt--and promise to keep them away from them painted-up gals and all that saloon whiskey!"

"It's against my better judgment, but I guess you win, Cole. Go pack your bags," his mother said.

9

Cole and Bold Eagle, mounted on their ponies, joined the other trail hands as they began to drive the three thousand head of longhorns down the Red Deer Creek. Cole was riding the tall chestnut gelding which had been a gift from Grandfather Jim. Bold Eagle was mounted on his new pony, also a gift from the Colonel, a black and white paint which had proven to be one of the best cow horses in the Ceebara remuda.

The Colonel had taken Bold Eagle to the horse remuda and allowed him to pick his own pony. He was pleased that the young Indian took his time before pointing to the black and white paint, "That one," he said, with finality.

"Good choice," Jim replied, as he loosed his lariat, handed it to Bold Eagle, and told him to catch the paint. Without hesitating, the young Indian made a loop, whirled it a couple of times over his head and quickly threw the loop around the pony's neck. It was amazing how easily he handled the lariat, but Jim had seen the two boys, spending hours practicing on the steers horns that were nailed to a board in the barn. Bold Eagle had learned well.

"What do you think we should name him?" he asked.

Looking the paint over closely, Bold Eagle answered, *"Badger!"*

"Good name," the Colonel responded, noticing the markings on the ponies head. "Kinda looks like a badger, don't he."

Jim was surprised at the ability of Quanah's son to ride the paint. Once mounted, he seemed to be a part of the horse, anticipating every move the horse made, and riding with such balance that he never reached for the horn of the saddle, no matter how sharp the horse turned when heading a steer.

"Those two boys are going to make top cowhands, some day," he said as Ned pulled his buckskin up beside the black.

Cole waved to his mother and grandmother who were standing on the veranda of the ranch house as he spurred his pony, *Comanche,* to head a large, spotted steer which was attempting to bolt from the herd. Kate turned her head and wiped a tear from her eye, realizing that her son was no longer a baby.

"You be careful, Cole, you hear!" she shouted as her son disappeared around the cottonwood grove.

Pepper, the camp cook, had taken the lead with his team of mules and chuck wagon. His real name was Stacey, but the cowboys had tacked the name of Pepper on him because he seasoned everything he cooked with a healthy dose of black pepper. Big Red, the huge longhorn steer which had led the first Ceebara herd from Waco, ten years before--with head down, sniffing the tracks of the mules--followed closely behind. The remainder of the herd, accepting Big Red as their leader, fell into step behind him.

This was Big Red's fourth trip up the trail to Dodge City,

having led three previous drives. Each time, he was given the comfort of a ride back to the ranch in a wagon made especially to carry his two thousand pound hulk back to his harem in Texas. He knew the trail better than any of the cowboys.

Colonel Cole, mounted on his aging black stallion, sat atop the highest hill to the south of the creek, and watched proudly as the cowboys quickly formed the herd into a compact group and headed them east down Red Deer Creek. About a days drive east, they would reach the Canadian River, cross it, and turn the herd north, following the well worn tracks of the Ceebara Trail--blazed by the first Ceebara herd in 1870--which led to the railroad at Dodge City.

The Colonel would not make this drive, leaving the responsibility of the herd in the hands of his young partner, Ned Armstrong. He would miss the trail, but realized that if he went along, the cowboys would look upon him as boss, and he wanted them to accept Ned in that capacity. And he knew that Ned could handle the task just as well.

The Kid sat his horse next to the Colonel and watched the huge herd head out. His bedroll and saddlebags were lashed behind his saddle, and he was ready to say goodbye to the Ceebara crew. It was time for him to head west to New Mexico Territory, where he had promised to ride for Mister Chisum. Reaching out, he took the left hand of Colonel Cole, shook it and said, "Colonel, I appreciate you taking me in and giving me a job, but I told you I couldn't stay the winter. Mister Chisum is expecting me, so I best say *adios* and be on my way. I'll drop by the ranch house and say my farewells to Miss Belle and Miss Kate. I'd like to come back some day, if you think you could use a good cowhand."

"There will always be a job for you on Ceebara, Kid," Jim said. "Anytime Chisum doesn't need you, just skeedaddle back here. You've made me a good hand."

"Thanks, Colonel, I reckon as how I'll just do that," the Kid said as he turned his horse and headed west.

The two youngsters, Cole and Bold Eagle, took their assigned positions on either side of Big Red and to his rear by fifty paces. The cattle fanned out behind them, forming an arrow head, with the big red steer as its point. Other cowboys rode along the side of the herd, keeping the cattle headed towards the lead steer. Drag riders brought up the rear, urging the stragglers forward so that they did not get separated from the huge herd.

The empty covered wagon, with its white canvas shining brightly in the early morning sunlight, pulled by a team of gray geldings, brought up the rear.

The Colonel watched until the entire procession disappeared around a bend in the creek. *Twelve days,* he thought, *and they should be pulling into the stock pens at Dodge City.*

Ned, riding his buckskin stallion, rode back and forth along the edges of the herd, shouting orders to some of the younger cowboys. "Watch it, Pete," he shouted to a red-headed cowboy, who was probably no older than seventeen and who had joined the Ceebara crew in early spring, "that pinto steer is fixin' to bolt. You got to out-think the critters or they'll outsmart you every time."

Sure enough, the steer headed into the brush along the creek bank and took two more with him. Pete tried to head them but was too late. They pushed their way into the middle of a large plum thicket and stopped, thinking they were hidden from the cowboy. But their horns gave them away--sticking above the thick foliage of the plum thicket. Pete, grudgingly, urged his horse into the thicket, realizing it was his responsibility to push the three animals back into the herd. Chaps and buckskins protected his body from the sharp branches of the plum thicket, but his hands and face didn't fare so well. When he finally pushed the steers out of their hiding place and back into the herd, he looked as if he had been in a wrestling match with a bobcat.

Ned, who had observed it all, shouted, "Until we get out of this creek bottom, you best keep your mind on them steers instead of thinking about them painted up gals you're going to court in the Longbranch. They ain't going to have nothing to do with a scratched up cowboy that lets dumbassed steers outthink him!"

Pete, embarrassed at his mistake, nodded his agreement.

Cole and Bold Eagle, with the easiest assignment at the head of the herd, after a couple of hours, began to get bored with their jobs. Just riding along on either side of Big Red wasn't exciting enough for a couple of ten year olds who thought a horse only had two speeds, running and whoa.

When a coyote jumped out of his den under Cole's pony and headed into the low hills surrounding the creek bottom, Cole kicked his horse into a run, chasing it. Immediately, the cattle on his side of the herd followed the horse.

Waddy, who was riding swing behind Cole's point position, shouted for the boy to pull up. Looking back, Cole could see that the herd was following him instead of Big Red, and realized his mistake. Waddy, rushing into the hole left by Cole, was able to turn the leaders back before the entire herd headed for the hills.

Cole turned his pony back and took his proper position at point just as Ned rode up. Even Bold Eagle, who was riding fifty yards to the right of Cole, flinched at the chewing Ned was giving Cole for leaving his position to chase a coyote.

"And tomorrow, you'll ride drag and eat dust all day-- maybe that will make you understand the importance of remaining in the position you're assigned," Ned shouted, as he headed back down the line of cowboys who were riding swing and flank.

After turning his horse away from Cole, Ned smiled to himself, thinking that when he was ten years old, he would have probably done the same thing. But he had to treat his son the same as he treated all of his cowboys, otherwise he would never learn the business.

Cole promised himself that he would never again disobey his father's orders. He definitely didn't want to take another chewing like he had just gotten. And he could imagine the ribbing he was going to have to take from the other cowboys as they sat around the campfire tonight! *"How about that coyote, Cole,"* they would say, *"did you get your loop on him?"* Or maybe they would say, *"I'll bet your ass is sore after that ass-chewing your Pa gave you today!"*

No sir-ee, he thought, *I ain't never going to run any-more coyotes!*

They reached the Canadian River before night, bedded the cattle, and made camp. Pepper soon had a large pot of coffee boiling over the campfire and was frying steaks for the hungry cowboys. A large pot of beans which he had cooked the night before was being warmed over the coals. As hungry as they were, the smell was almost more than Cole and Bold Eagle could bear.

The other cowboys, once their horses were unsaddled and rubbed down, made the coffee pot their first stop, dipping tin cups into the strong brew, blowing across the tops of the cups and sipping the steaming liquid.

Although the two ten-year-olds had never had coffee before, it only seemed fair, now that they were full-fledged cowboys, to do all the things that the older cowboys were doing. They each took a tin cup from the chuck wagon, dipped it into the boiling brew, and proceeded to place the edge of the cup to their lips. Both boys screamed in pain as the hot edge of the cup burned their lips.

Smiling, Manuel said, as he dipped his cup into the coffee pot, "*Este coffee is mucho caliente.*You got to blow, first, boys," then proceeded to demonstrate. Blowing across the brim of the cup, then placing the cup next to his lips, but not touching the lips, he sucked as hard as he had blown as he tipped the cup towards his mouth. The very top of the coffee, cooled from the blowing and sucking, was pulled into his mouth without the cup ever touching his lips.

The boys tried again, and successfully pulled a small amount of the black brew into their mouths. They really didn't like the taste, but smiled and smacked, imitating the other cowboys, and continued to nurse the coffee until Pepper shouted, "Come and get it, you mangy bunch of saddle tramps, 'afore I throw it out to the coyotes."

When Ned walked up to Cole and placed his arm around the boy's shoulder and squeezed, in an indication of forgiveness of his days misadventure, Cole apologized.

"Pa, I'm sorry--I promise I won't ever leave my position again," he said. Bold Eagle said nothing, but was thinking he was certainly glad that the coyote hadn't jumped from under his horse!

The two young boys lined up with the other cowboys, filled their plates to overflowing, and came back for seconds. "Lordee," Pepper, looking very serious, said, "I don't know how two small stomachs can hold so much," as he filled their plates again.

The next morning, Ned prepared to take the herd across the river. The Canadian was running three feet deep and was two hundred yards across, the result of a heavy thunderstorm upstream. As a precaution, he had two of the cowboys tie lariats to the chuck wagon and wade their horses upstream from the wagon as the mules pulled it across the river. Good thinking, on his part, because the water was deep enough to float the chuck wagon. The lariats kept it stabilized and headed in the proper direction.

The empty supply wagon was crossed in the same manner. Next, Big Red was pushed into the stream and made straight for the wagons on the opposite shore. His herd followed faithfully. The horse remuda was the last to cross.

With everyone safely on the north shore of the river, Ned shouted to move them out, and Pepper slapped the mules on the rump with the reins as he yelled for them to "giddyap, ya flop-eared ornery critters".

Then he "hee'd and hawed" them to the right and to the left around the sand dunes along the river's banks, blazing a trail for Big Red to follow.

The big red steer followed obediently, leading the herd on the second day of the drive to Dodge City.

* * * * * * * *

The morning of the third day started out as usual, with Pepper breaking covers about four a.m., starting his fires and putting the coffee on to boil. The Dutch Oven was greased and sourdough biscuits were patted out and put into place to start their rise. Steaks were cut from a steer's hindquarter which was wrapped in burlap in the back of the chuck wagon. Yesterday's left-over beans were dragged out of hiding in the many pots and pans of the chuck wagon, a healthy supply of water poured in, and the pot was placed over the coals to start to heat.

The smell of coffee boiling was enough to start bedrolls moving and sleepy-eyed cowboys setting up and putting their hats on their heads. A cowboy's hat was the first thing he reached for after awakening in the morning.

Cole was no different, he was always the first up, the first to grab his hat and the first to tilt the coffee pot over his tin cup. Everything about this cattle drive was a new experience for him, and he didn't want to waste a second or miss a thing that might happen while he was asleep.

He kicked the bedroll next to his and said, "Come on, Chief, we're burning daylight. Get out of that sack!"

Jim Bold Eagle was too long a name for a cattle drover, so Cole had placed the nickname of *Chief* on him. Soon, all the other trail hands were doing the same.

The two boys were the first in line to fill their plates and the first to head for the horse remuda to catch their horses. Ned had told them they were to be treated no different than any of the other trail hands. "You'll catch your own horses and do your own saddling," he said, "and when you quit for the day, you'll rub your horse down and see that he gets a bait of oats before you turn him in with the rest of the remuda."

This morning there was a little nip in the air as a result of a weak cold front passing through during the night. The horses reacted to the cool air with a little more energy. *Comanche*, Cole's Chestnut gelding, had accepted Cole as his friend and master, and had never offered to buck, so Cole never expected him to react any differently today. He was, however, in for a surprise.

As Cole approached the remuda, he called out his pony's name. "Come on Comanche, time to saddle up."

Comanche's reaction was to first paw the ground, kicking up a cloud of dust, then he kicked up his rear legs and bolted to the back of the horse herd. Cole followed him, uncoiled his rope and threw it accurately over the horse's head.

As the rope settled around his neck, Comanche froze, then waited for Cole to hand-walk up the rope, all the time watching him with a mischievous eye. "What's the matter with you, this morning, boy?" Cole asked, as he pulled the bits into the horses mouth and the leather bridle over his ears.

Comanche stood still as Cole rubbed the night's dust off his back, placed the blanket and threw the saddle on. Cinching it up tight, he mounted. Everything was fine until he touched his spurs to the horse's side.

Comanche, still with a mischievous glint in his eye, turned his head just enough to look Cole in the eye, then kicked both hind feet about six feet into the air. As his rear feet hit the ground, his front feet left the ground, he bowed in the middle and reached for the sky.

Most of the other cowboys had reached the remuda and were shaking out their ropes when Cole's rodeo began. "Ride him, Cole," they shouted, laughing at the turn of events.

Ned was as surprised as Cole at Comanche's reaction, and under his breath, said to himself, "Lord, don't let him get hurt."

Well, Cole was surprised, but even though he was just ten years old, going on eleven, he had spent about seven of those years in the saddle and reacted quickly to the situation. He shoved his boots deep into the stirrups, squeezed his knees into the pommels of the saddle, took a tight hold on the reins and relaxed.

Comanche, jumped, kicked, reared and ran but Cole held his seat and never grabbed leather. About six jumps later, Comanche stopped dead in his tracks, looked back once again at his friend and master who was still seated in the saddle, and if horses could smile, he smiled.

Ned walked up to Cole and said, "That was a fine ride, son, I'm proud of you. You rode old Comanche like a bronc rider. Where'd you learn that?"

Cole smiled, and answered, "Me and the Chief, we been riding some of the colts when no one else was around. Some of them buck pretty good. Why'd you reckon Comanche acted this way, Pa?"

"Change of weather, son. Horses get to feeling their oats on cold mornings, and some of the gentlest will put a hump in their backs just because they feel good. Just always remember, anything can happen when you put your weight in the saddle for the first time in the morning."

All of the other cowboys made a point to walk over to Cole, pat him on the leg and tell him what a great ride he made. Cole's chest nearly popped the buttons on his shirt.

* * * * * * *

As Ned headed his herd towards Dodge City, another herd was entering the stockyards from the west. It was a small herd, only eleven hundred head, but they were fat and slick, indicating they had not been on the trail for very many days.

Several buyers sat on the top rail of the corral fence and watched as the cowboys pushed the herd in and closed the gate.

"Good looking herd," one of the buyers said to another. "First time I've seen that brand. Where you reckon they're from?"

"Don't know," the second buyer answered, "but couldn't be far, as much flesh as they're carrying. Brand looks like a Zero Cross Triangle on the left hip. Don't remember ever seeing that before."

A big, bull of a man, riding a large sorrel gelding, dismounted and walked towards the buyers. His face was covered with a mat of black whiskers, and his entire body, from the top of his hat to the bottom of his boots, was covered with a film of fine dust. He wore one Colt revolver, hung low on his right hip and carried a repeating Winchester rifle in his left hand.

"Howdy," he said, as he looked straight at the two buyers.

"Hello," the buyers answered. "Fine looking herd you got there."

"Thanks. Just brought 'em in from New Mexico. Got a ranch over west of the Rabbit Ears. Name's Borne, Henry Borne, but most folks just call me Dutch."

"Say, I've heard of you," the first buyer said as he dismounted from the fence rail and stuck out his hand. "Long is my name--John Long. Was you the same Borne that got caught with them other buffalo hunters at Adobe Walls when Quanah Parker's Comanches attacked?"

At first, Dutch thought Long was going to say he had heard about the *outlaw* Dutch Henry. He relaxed, smiled and took Long's hand and squeezed. Long grimaced as the huge hand locked on his with an iron grip. "I reckon as how I am. But I ain't a buffaler hunter no more. I bought me some cows and started a ranch over in New Mexico Territory. Not too far from that Dorsey feller's ranch."

"Name's Abercrombie--what you call that brand?" the other buyer said, as he shook hands with Dutch, "First time I've ever seen it."

"Circle Cross Triangle," Dutch said, with a touch of anger in his voice. "The reason you ain't never seen it is because I ain't never sold any of my herd before. Just got it started a couple of years ago."

"Well, Mr. Borne, how about me buying you a drink at the Long Branch, and see if we can make a deal on that herd. I got some empty rail cars and need about that many head to fill 'em up," Long said.

"How about meeting me there in about an hour," Dutch replied, "I've got a terrible thirst built up, but I need to find a room and a bath before I start getting tanked up."

"That will be fine," Long said.

Abercrombie spoke as Dutch turned to walk towards the Dodge House, "Better give me a chance to bid on 'em before you make a deal with that old scalawag. He don't ever want to pay top dollar."

"I'll do that," Dutch replied, turned and walked away.

Abercrombie walked back to the corral and climbed to the top rail, marveling at the fat that was on this herd. "Better shape than anything that's come in this year," he said. Then, looking at the brand on a big steer that was standing near him, he mused, "Something familiar about that brand. Seems like I may have seen it before, but guess not--Borne said it's the first herd he's sold."

* * * * * * * *

At the same time that Dutch Henry pushed his herd into the corrals at Dodge City, a group of twelve loaded wagons pulled out, crossed the Arkansas River and headed south down the Ceebara Trail. The wagons, belonging to Ed Jones and Joe Plummer, were loaded with supplies for the new settlement in the Texas Panhandle, Hidetown and Fort Elliot. After delivering the supplies, the wagons would be filled with newly acquired buffalo hides and returned to the railroad at Dodge City.

Three more wagons, loaded with a more precious cargo, pulled in behind the supply wagons. The three wagons, each pulled by a team of fat mules, were driven by women--and the precious cargo they were carrying were twelve pretty dance hall girls and all of their belongings, four in each wagon. Describing them as dance hall girls was using the term very loosely--actually the word *prostitutes* would have described them better.

A new saloon was opening in Hidetown to supplement the eleven which were already operating at full steam in the buffalo hunters metropolis, and the girls were hired by the new owner to entertain the hunters. With twelve saloons operating in a town of no more than three hundred people, the ones with the prettiest girls were the ones that would draw the most trade. Of course, there were times when the population swelled to over a thousand, when the hunters brought in their hides. It looked as if this new establishment was going to draw the biggest crowds.

One of the girls was a beautiful Louisiana girl, that the cowboys who had trailed their herds into Dodge City from Texas called Frenchy. No one new her real name, and it didn't really matter. Most of the *painted ladies* of Dodge City didn't care to tell their real names, going by such monikers as Squirrel Tooth Alice, Big Nose Kate and Big Emma. Frenchy, so named because of her Louisiana background and her ability to speak French, had heard that to the south of Dodge City about one hundred and thirty miles, buffalo hunters had set up a hide trading center on the banks of the Sweetwater Creek and were swarming into the center like flies to a molasses lick. The army had also established a fort within shouting distance of the hide hunters camp--with about three hundred woman-hungry soldiers within its walls.

Buffalo hunters with pockets full of gold after selling their hides, and soldiers with no place to spend their pay checks, was an ideal place for Frenchy and the other girls to peddle their wares!

The supply wagon's crew, after a long layover in the wild frontier town of Dodge City, was broke. They had already spent all of their money on whiskey and women, and kept away from the three wagons loaded with the women when camp was made at night. After three days on the trail, however, some of the more bold drivers, began approaching the women with all kinds of offers of help--building their campfires, harnessing their mules, and filling their water barrels at water crossings.

Some of the more frail ladies succumbed to the offers of

barter, and were soon sharing their bedrolls with the teamsters--but not Frenchy. The only barter she was interested in was gold coin. One evening, a huge driver with long, dirty, unkempt hair and whiskers that covered a scar-mocked face decided that the beautiful lady from Louisiana would be his bed mate for the night.

Grabbing Frenchy by the arm, he started dragging her away into the darkness surrounding the campfire. He didn't, however, reckon with her courage. Suddenly, he screamed with pain as she took his little finger in her mouth and bit down. Releasing his hold on her wrist, he slapped at her with his other hand. But the agile dance hall girl ducked the huge hand and at the same time pulled a small Derringer from beneath the folds of her dress, aimed and fired, creasing the teamster's skull just above his right ear. The force of the small bullet knocked the man backwards and he fell moaning next to the fire.

Frenchy disappeared into the darkness and watched as the attempted rapist was helped to his feet by fellow drivers and ushered back to the supply wagons. She replaced the small pistol into the folds of her dress and returned to the fire, where the other girls congratulated her on her success.

"Maybe that'll teach them to respect our wishes," one of the older girls said as she held Frenchy close and patted her back.

* * * * * * * *

The Ceebara herd continued to travel slowly to the north, making about twelve miles each day. On the fifth day, early in the afternoon, they reached the North Fork of the Canadian River.

Calling Slim to his side, Ned gave instructions to cross the river before dark and bed the herd down on the north side of the river. "I don't like the looks of that cloud building in the southwest. Could put the river on the rise before morning."

Slim nodded in agreement and took the lead, motioning for Pepper to follow him with the chuck wagon. Big Red and the herd followed obediently. Water in the river was no more than ankle deep on the horses and the crossing was made without incident.

After allowing the cattle to drink, Ned pushed the herd to high ground a half mile north of the river, where the cowboys circled them and allowed them to spread out and start grazing on the lush grass.

Looking to the east, Ned noticed a group of wagons making camp about a mile down river, the first they had seen since leaving Ceebara headquarters. "Those wagons are going to be in a heap of trouble if the river rises during the night," he told Slim. "I think I'll ride down and see who's in charge."

Cole and Jim Bold Eagle rode up as Ned turned his buckskin towards the wagon camp downstream. Motioning to the two boys, he shouted, "Might as well come along, Cole, we'll see what those wagons are carrying--might have some licorice sticks for boys like you."

With no danger of Indians in the area, the wagons were not circled, but were parked haphazardly along the river's banks, each finding shade beneath the huge cottonwood trees.

Ned rode slowly by each and watched as mules were unhooked, their harness removed, and hobbles placed on their front feet to allow them to graze on the tender grass without straying too far from the campground. He stopped when he came to the lead wagon, where a tall freighter was giving orders to the others.

"Howdy," Ned said, pulling the buckskin up next to the freighter.

"Howdy," the freighter responded, extending his hand. "Name's Timberlake, most folks just call me Tex."

"Ned Armstrong, Tex--and these two buttons are my boys, Cole and Bold Eagle."

Bold Eagle sat a little straighter in the saddle when Ned referred to him as *his boy*--made him feel more accepted.

Tex looked the boys over, smiled, and nodded his head in greeting.

"Looks like you got a sizable herd, Ned--headed for Dodge?"

"Yep, a little over three thousand head. Brought them up from our ranch south of the Canadian. Been on the trail about five days."

"That the Ceebara spread that this here trail is named after?"

"I reckon that's right. We brought our first herd up in '70. Since then the army and buffalo hunters have been using it to find their way to Hidetown on the Sweetwater. I guess the name *Ceebara Trail* just kinda stuck with it."

"These wagons and supplies belong to Jones and Plummer, merchants in Dodge City. We're headed to Hidetown where we'll sell the supplies and load the wagons with hides and tongues and bring them back to the railroad at Dodge," Tex said.

"I don't mean to be interfering," Ned said, as he dismounted. "But if that cloud back in the west keeps building, your wagons are going to be in a heap of trouble when the rain starts. I've seen these plains' streams turn from a trickle to a roaring torrent in a matter of hours when one of these thunderbusters dump four or five inches of rain. You'd be safer if you camped up on the ridge."

Tex, anger showing in his eyes, replied, "That cloud don't look too bad to me. It would take a helluva flood to put this little old stream out of its banks. I 'spect we'll just stay where we are, that ways we don't have to tote our water so far."

Ned could see that it would do no good to argue with him, so he remounted and rode on down the string of loaded wagons, speaking to the teamsters as he rode by. He was surprised when he reached the last three wagons and discovered they were occupied by a group of women.

The women were standing around, their mules still hitched to the wagons, waiting on the men in the freight wagons to come to their assistance. Ned tipped his hat and spoke.

"Howdy, ladies. Danged if you ain't the purtiest mule skinners I ever did see," he said with a smile.

They all spoke as one as they stepped towards his horse, "Hello, Cowboy--why don't y'all step down off them horses and visit awhile."

Ned suspected they weren't the average frontier ladies, headed back to their husbands and kids out on the wild frontier. It was plain to see that they wore too much lipstick and rouge--and their dresses were cut a way too low at the top and too high at the bottom to be somebody's mother.

Cole and Bold Eagle looked them over and blushed when

one of the younger girls winked at them and patted her rear.

Ned smiled at their embarrassment and made his introductions. "My name's Ned Armstrong and these two cowboys are Cole and Bold Eagle. We're taking our herd up the trail to Dodge City and thought we'd check to see what this wagon train is all about."

The older lady of the group smiled and said, "Nice to meet you, Ned. Most folks just call me Pearl, and these girls are my wards. We're headed for Hidetown where we intend to entertain the boys-- for a fee, of course. Looks to me like you could use a little entertaining, yourself."

"Sorry, ladies," Ned replied, "My wife might frown on me seeking entertainment elsewhere. And these boys are probably going to need to wait four or five years before they would appreciate the kind of music y'all make."

The girls all looked sad at this statement, and one of them shouted. "What about them other cowboys we seen herding them cows? I bet they could use a little entertaining."

Smiling, Ned said, "I'll see if I can twist their arms and send them over. But before you unharness them mules, you'd best move back up on higher ground. I think we're in for some wet weather, and you may find your wagons floating in the morning if you remain here on the river bank."

Just then, Frenchy, who had been behind one of the wagons, stepped into the open. Ned gasped, as if he had seen a ghost. Regaining his composure, he said, "Well I be danged-- Jeannie Boudreaux!"

Frenchy, stopped, looked at him in puzzlement, then recognized the young cowboy from Kentucky that she had met in Waco at the Longhorn Saloon, danced with, and made love to, ten years ago.

"Well, if it ain't Ned Armstrong. I never thought I'd be seeing you again--especially out here in the middle of this God forsaken country, ten thousand miles from nowhere!"

Ned dismounted and nervously took her hand in his and allowed as how it was good to see her again. She smiled, leaned forward and whispered, "Name's Elizabeth McGraw, Ned. That name Jeannie Boudreaux was just the one I was using in Waco. I'd just as soon you'd forget both of them. Everyone calls me Frenchy, and that suits me fine."

"Alright, Frenchy it is," Ned said.

Turning to the other girls, Frenchy said, in her pleasant Southern drawl, "Girls, this here is an old friend that I met down the trail a few years back--best damned dancer this side of New Orleans." Then, turning back to Ned, she asked, "How's the Colonel and his wife Belle making out? Seems to me I remember she had a couple of kids when they got married in Waco before y'all headed them 'horns up the trail."

"Colonel's doing well--a little older and a little more ornery. Belle's still pretty as ever--and I married her daughter Kate. That sprout sitting there on that Chestnut gelding is our son, Cole. Cole, light down off that horse and shake hands with an old friend, Frenchy."

Cole slipped easily to the ground, and as he had been taught, removed his hat and took Frenchy's hand, shaking it awkwardly. "Pleased to meet you, Miss Frenchy," he said.

"And that young brave, sitting that paint horse is the son of the great Comanche Chief, Quanah Parker--Jim Bold Eagle Parker. Both these boys are namesakes of the Colonel," Ned added.

Bold Eagle remained on his horse, but smiled and nodded to Frenchy.

After a short conversation, Ned remounted and said they'd best get back to the herd, once again cautioning the women to move to higher ground, pointing to a small knoll no more than a hundred yards back of the river's bank. As they rode away, he was pleased to see that the women had taken his advice.

"Pa," Cole asked, as they rode back towards the herd, "Was them *painted up ladies* that I keep hearing the cowboys talk about?"

"I guess you could call them that," Ned answered.

"And was Miss Frenchy a *painted up lady*, too?"

Without looking at Cole, Ned answered, "Yep."

"Then how'd you come about knowing a *painted up lady*, Pa?" Cole asked.

The conversation was getting a little unpleasant for Ned, and he would just as soon change the subject. "I met her a long time ago, even before I met your Ma. She's a friend. Would you look at that cloud, boys! She's building fast, a lot of wind in her, too. See how it's rolling from bottom to top--and black as the Ace of Spades! We best hurry, it's liable to be raining by the time we get back to the herd."

He kicked the buckskin into a lope, thankful to put an end to the questions.

* * * * * * * *

Pepper had his camp made, a fire going and coffee boiling when Ned and the boys slid their horses to a stop next to the chuck wagon. Most of the cattle were grazing leisurely along the top of the ridge except for forty or fifty which were still taking on water in the middle of the stream. Most of the cowboys had ridden in and were standing around the fire. A few large drops of rain began to fall and a cold wind had shifted off the cloud.

"Let's get mounted up, boys, looks like we're in for a blow. Circle the herd and hold your ground just in case they decide to head back to the ranch," Ned instructed.

"Pa, what's that?" Cole shouted as he pointed towards the black cloud. "Looks like a big snake coming down out of the cloud!"

"It's a cyclone, son! Forget the cows, men! Find a low spot and take shelter, looks like it's heading right down the middle of the river!"

Riding close to Cole and Bold Eagle, he motioned for them to follow and spurred his buckskin towards a shallow wash he had spotted back towards the wagon train. Pulling to a stop, he dismounted and shouted for the boys to do the same, released his horse and flattened himself on the ground in the bottom of the wash. The boys fell to the ground, one on each side of Ned and he placed his arms around them for protection.

The air was filled with the terrible roar of the twister as it snaked down the middle of the river, kicking up sand and brush, and now and then pulling the water from the small stream. Ned watched as it changed direction, jumping from the stream bed to the banks of the river, then heading for Pepper's campground.

His heart pounded as he watched the base of the twister, a hundred yards across, turn once again and slant towards the river. The chuck wagon was spared, as the snarling snake passed within inches of the tongue and sucked Pepper's campfire and coffee pot into the air.

A deluge of rain and hail was now pelting Ned and the boys as the twister turned in their direction. "Keep down! Keep down," he shouted as Cole tried to find protection from the hail. He pulled both boys tightly to his side and waited as the cyclone passed directly overhead. He heard, and even felt the earth tremble, as something large fell from the air no more than six feet from where they lay. It was one of the large steers which had been drinking from the stream, twisted and mangled with its neck broken.

The small depression protected them from the brunt of the storm, and it passed over as quickly as it had come. The wind calmed somewhat, but the rain and hail didn't stop. Rain was coming in sheets and water began to rise in the wash where they lay.

Pulling the boys up, he dragged them towards the chuck wagon and motioned for them to find shelter under its bed. Looking to the right, he could see the cowboys begin to appear from another wash, two hundred yards up the ridge from the camp. There were no horses in sight.

The rain was falling in sheets and it was not possible to see if the cattle had stampeded. The only thing they could do was huddle under the chuck wagon and the flatbed wagon and wait for the storm to pass. For two hours the rain continued to fall, and the river continued to rise. Then they heard a roar, making them think that another twister was approaching--but it was not the roar of the wind, it was the roar of the water as a four foot head of water, carrying trees and brush rushed past.

Even Ned's precaution to make camp above the river was barely enough to keep the water from sweeping the wagons away as the roaring water pushed its way out of the river's banks--the teamsters wagons, if they had escaped the twister, would not be so fortunate.

Suddenly, the rain stopped and within minutes the sun, low on the western horizon, began to break through the clouds. Crawling from under the wagons, Ned instructed the men to try to find their horses before dark, forget the cattle, and ride to the aid of the wagon train, for he feared the worst for their safety.

Luckily, the saddled horses had only strayed a short distance and most were unhurt, standing under the protection of a small cottonwood grove a quarter of a mile from camp. However, Ned's buckskin, Cole's chestnut, and Bold Eagle's paint were nowhere in sight.

Walking down the path of the storm towards the wagon train, Ned and the boys found several head of dead cattle, twisted and mangled from the storm's fury. Then, as if by a miracle, the three horses were spotted off to the left of the trail, muddy from head to foot. It was plain to see that the storm had picked them up, carried them a short distance, set them down and rolled them in the mud--but had broken no bones.

"Thank God," Ned said as he whistled to his buckskin. The horse turned his head towards the sound and nickered, waiting for Ned to arrive.

After looking the horses over and determining that they were alright, Ned and the boys brushed the mud from the saddles, mounted and rode towards the wagon train. The rest of the crew followed.

The wagon train campground was a shambles. The only wagons left were those of the women, which were parked above the roaring river. One of them was overturned and its contents were spilled along the hillside. The women were standing around, soaked and crying. Their mules, although un-hitched, were still harnessed and were standing a short distance from the wagons. The storm had hit before the men had time to come to the aid of the ladies.

Looking downstream, Ned could see three or four men crawling up the river's banks. Further down a dozen or so mules were floundering out of the water. Supplies from the vanished wagons were scattered along the storm's path for as far as the eye could see.

"Are any of the ladies hurt?" he questioned Frenchy, who had run to his horse when he arrived.

"Just scratches and bruises," she replied, "but the men, where are the men?"

Shaking his head, Ned said, "Looks like the storm must have gotten most of them. I see a few downstream that are still alive. We'll just have to hope for the best."

Crying, Frenchy said, "We watched as the cyclone came down the river and it hit the supply wagons head on. You can't believe it, Ned! It just lifted the wagons, men, mules and eve-rything and they disappeared into the funnel. Then when the water came, what little was left was swept away downriver."

"Slim, you and Waddy and Sonny see if you can right that overturned wagon and help the ladies gather up their plunder. Cole, you and Bold Eagle stay here and help--gather some wood and see if you can't get a fire started. The rest of you men, follow me--spread out and we'll see if we can find any of the mule skinners," Ned instructed as he put spurs to the buckskin's side and headed downstream along the storm's path.

The men he had seen crawling from the water were sitting dazed on the river bank. When he asked them if they had seen any more of the drivers, they shook their heads no, without answering. Ned continued downstream.

One of his cowboys, riding along the ridge to his left, shouted, "Here's a couple of them, boss,--pretty banged up but looks like they're still alive."

"Do what you can for them, Joe, and help them back to the women's wagons," Ned replied.

Riding on, Ned soon spotted three of the drivers, drowned and lodged in a brush drift next to the river's bank. Two dead mules were lodged in the same drift. Although they rode for two miles downstream, they never found the other mule skinners nor the wagon train cook.

"Let's head back, men," Ned shouted. It's going to be dark before long and we need to get some kind of camp made before night. "We'll make another search in the morning."

Pepper had taken a span of the ladies' mules to the cow camp, hooked them to his chuck wagon, and brought the chuck wagon back to the three remaining wagons. Cole and Bold Eagle had gathered a large pile of cottonwood limbs and Pepper had a roaring fire going next to his chuck wagon. The women were huddled around the fire trying to get warm and dry.

Using the women's coffee pot, he had pulled a few of the coals away from the large fire and had a pot of coffee boiling.

The ladies had spread their bedrolls out to dry around the fire, and Pepper was cutting steaks from the hindquarter of a beef he had stored in the chuck wagon.

As night closed in, everyone was chewing on a steak, somewhat rare but tasty. Standing around the campfire, everyone was anxious to tell their experiences of weathering the storm. The five surviving mule skinners, amazingly were only bruised, and told a harrowing tale of how the twister had pulled them into the air, whirled them around with mules, wagons, supplies and debris, and dropped them a quarter of a mile from where they had camped.

Their conversation was interrupted by a sound coming from the darkness surrounding the fire. "Hello, the camp!" Then two more of the mule skinners stepped forward from the darkness, clothes torn half off, and one holding a broken arm.

"Lord have mercy," Pearl screamed, when she recognized one of the drivers as being the one who had shared her bed the night before. "Jake, I never thought I'd see your ugly face again!"

* * * * * * * *

"Sonny, take half the crew and check on the cows," Ned instructed the next morning. "Miguel, you take Cole and Bold Eagle and locate our mules and horse remuda. Slim, take the rest of the crew and scout down river for more survivors. Me and these bruised up mule skinners will pull those poor souls out of that brush pile and bury them."

Turning to Pearl, he asked, "How many men are missing?"

"As well as I remember, there was fourteen all together, counting the cook and Timberlake. We got seven alive and three dead in that brush pile, which means there's still four missing," Pearl replied.

"You hear that, Slim? You'll be looking for four more. Let's hope you find them alive."

While Ned and one of the mule skinners waded out to the brush pile and tied ropes on the three drowned men, the other wagon drivers dug a shallow grave in the sand next to the water's edge. Ned made a dally with the rope around his saddle horn, and spoke to the buckskin. The horse pulled and the bodies came free from the tangled brush and were pulled to shore.

Ned stopped the horse next to the grave, the gravediggers loosened the rope and rolled the bodies into the grave. "Cover them over, boys," he said. "We'll say a word over them tomorrow. Right now we got more pressing things to do."

After the burial, Ned rode back to the cow camp, where some of the cowboys had just returned with their mules and most of the horse remuda. Waddy pulled up, removed his hat and wiped the sweat from his brow. "Looks like all the cattle are accounted for, boss. We lost forty head to the twister but the others are still where we put them, enjoying the rest."

"That's good, Waddy. See if you can get 'em bunched. Soon as Slim returns from his search we might as well move 'em out. No use in burning any more daylight around here. We're still seven days out of Dodge, and now we're going to be seeing after those ladies and their three wagons as well as all of the mules we can locate."

Riding back to the wagon train campground, he told Pepper and the ladies about his plans. "Cole, you and Bold Eagle help these ladies get their mules harnessed and hooked to their wagons. We can't be leaving them out here by themselves, and we can't turn the herd around to guide them back to Hidetown--they'll have to return to Dodge with us."

The ladies didn't argue. After the ordeal with the twister

they were not about to try to continue on to Hidetown without an escort. They began to pack and load their bedrolls on the wagons, and gathered the wet clothing which they had hung on nearby bushes to dry.

Slim soon returned, leading a dozen mules which he had found along the river bottom, but reported that they hadn't seen *hide nor hair* of the missing men.

10

The remaining trip to Dodge passed uneventfully. However, seven days on the trail with twenty young cowboys escorting three thousand head of longhorns and twelve pretty *ladies of the night*, resulted in some very close relationships between the cowboys and the ladies. Upon reaching the outskirts of Dodge City, the cowboys had a look of contentment on their faces, even though they had spent much of their bonus money before ever reaching the saloons of the frontier town.

Dodge City had grown considerably since the first Ceebara herd had trailed up from the *Llano Estacado,* but the growth had only made it wilder and rougher. There were now seventeen saloons and dance halls, over a thousand prostitutes, hundreds of gamblers--most of them crooked-- and thieves and pimps by the hundreds.

During the three year period of 1872, 1873, and 1874, over three million buffalo hides had been piled and shipped from the railhead at Dodge City. With hides bringing from three to six dollars each, hunters had brought a lot of money into the small town which was known to have little or no law. Add to that, the influx of the many trail drives from Texas bringing up as many as two hundred thousand head of cattle in one year. A river of gold was flowing into the town, and with it came the "gold miners" to mine what they could, honestly or dishonestly. No wonder that sin and crime ran rampant.

Dodge City had become known throughout the west as the "wickedest little city in America." A newspaper article in the Hays, Kansas Sentinel reported:

"Dodge is the Deadwood of Kansas, her incorporate limits are the rendezvous of all the unemployed scallawagism in seven States; her principal business is polygamy without the sanction of religion; her code of morals is the honor of thieves, and decency she knows not. Dodge is a fast town. The employment of many citizens is gambling, her virtue is prostitution and her beverage is whiskey. She is a merry town, and the only visible means of support of a great number of her citizens is jocularity. Her rowdyism has taken its most aggravated form ... Seventeen saloons furnish inspiration, and many people become inspired--not to say drunk. Every facility is afforded for the exercise of conviviality, and no restriction is placed on licentiousness.

"The town is full of prostitutes and every other house is a brothel....the street is brilliantly lighted and thronged with gaudily dressed women, and men whose garb betokens the cowboy."

The Washington Evening Star described Dodge City of the times:

"Dodge City is a wicked little town...the Texas cattle drovers loiter and dissipate sometime for months, and share the boughten dalliances of fallen women."

It was to this Dodge City that Ned had brought twenty cowboys, three thousand head of longhorns--and two small boys who had never been in a town in their life.

After penning the herd in the corrals next to the railroad, Ned walked to the office of Jones and Plummer with the surviving members of the wagon train. "It was a terrible tragedy, Mr. Plummer," he said. "We did all we could after the storm to try to locate the missing men and mules, but were unsuccessful. It is my opinion that they were all drowned and washed down the river. We brought in two dozen mules, most of them got a few cuts and bruises but no broken bones."

"I appreciate all that you have done, Mr. Armstrong," Plummer replied. "I'll send a crew down immediately to see if we can locate them, and salvage what we can of the supplies. Hidetown is going to be expecting those supplies, so I will send another shipment. The ladies can trail along with their wagons if they so wish."

After checking in at the Dodge House and getting a room, Ned and the two boys took a much needed bath, then walked to the office of the Great Western Livestock Company, where his old friend, Vince Abercrombie was head buyer.

"Ned!" Abercrombie shouted, "Come in! You're a sight for sore eyes. I was afraid something might have happened and you wasn't going to bring a herd in this year."

Ned smiled, took his hand, and replied. "Good to see you, Mr. Abercrombie. I'd like for you to meet a couple of my sidekicks, my son, Cole, and his friend Jim Bold Eagle. This is their first cattle drive, and I must say, they made pretty good hands."

"Pleased to meet you, boys," Abercrombie said, taking their hands and shaking them as he would if they had been grown men. This put a smile on both of their faces--looks like they are real cowboys, now.

"So, how's the Colonel, Miss Belle and Miss Kate?" he asked.

"Doing fine, Mr. Abercrombie. Colonel sends his regards and says if I don't squeeze a good price for our herd out of you, he's going to skin me alive when I return."

Abercrombie laughed, then looked solemn. "Market's kinda depressed right now, Ned. Been a lot of herds brought in this year, and the financial crunch back east has put a damper on sales. But I know your cattle--they're always in better shape than anything we get in from Central Texas--and I guarantee you top dollar."

"Can't ask any more than that, Mr. Abercrombie, but you know I'm going to be scouting around to make certain that it *is* top dollar."

"Now, Ned, you know you'd be wasting your time. I've always bought every head you've brought in, and paid more than any of the other buyers have offered. It breaks my heart to think that you would think I'd try to skin you," Abercrombie said, with a twinkle in his eye.

Ned smiled, "Sure, you've always paid top dollar--after we've threatened to take the herd back to Texas. You ain't no different than any of the other thieves that call themselves cow buyers. You'd skin your own mother if you thought you could make a dime."

The two boys sat listening to this good natured bickering, thinking that Abercrombie must be one of the most dishonest men in the cattle business.

"Well, why don't we take a look at that mangy bunch of moss backs that you brought in. Probably cut your herd and brought the sorriest ones to market and expect me to pay top dollar for them."

"No, sir!" Cole spoke up, not liking for the cow buyer to insinuate that they were dishonest. "We didn't bring the sorriest ones. Grandpa said we's to bring the best. He said we have a reputation to keep up, and he didn't want anyone saying our herd wasn't the best!"

Abercrombie laughed. "Now don't go getting your dandruff up, young man. I was just joshing your pa. I know him and the Colonel always send the best. But you got to understand, the folks I work for out of Chicago expect me to buy 'em just as cheap as I can get 'em. Let's go take a look."

Abercrombie retrieved his hat from the hat rack and they followed him out the door, down the dirt street and to the stock pens. Climbing the fence for a better look, the buyer whistled, "Seems like they get a little better every year, Ned. Carrying more flesh, too."

"We been culling our bulls, Mr. Abercrombie, and our cows have been dropping better calves. Colonel says he's going to try to get us some of those Durham bulls out of England to cross-breed to our longhorn cows. He thinks that will put more meat on them and still have an animal that will be easy to keep."

"I've heard some of these Texans coming up the Chisholm trail saying the same thing. That should please the home office if we can send them a little more flesh and a little less bone."

"Well, what do you think, Mr. Abercrombie, now that you've seen them--like to make a bid?"

"No, Ned, I tell you what I'm going to do. You scout around and see what the other buyers are willing to pay and I'll give you half a cent a pound more than their top bid. Looks to me like they're going to press the scales around a thousand pounds each, so that'll give you an extra five dollars a head."

"Fair enough, Mr. Abercrombie. I'll ask around."

Changing the subject and looking more serious, Abercrombie said, "Ned, I bought another herd about two weeks ago, almost as good as these. We sprained one of the steer's knees when we were loading them so I cut him back until he mends up. Got him in another pen down by the railroad water tower. If you've got time, I'd like for you to take a look at him."

"Sure, Mr. Abercrombie, be glad to," Ned said, thinking that the buyer wanted his advice on how to doctor the knee.

They walked the short distance to the water tower, climbed the fence and watched as the steer limped towards them, thinking they were going to throw him some hay.

"Don't look too bad, Mr. Abercrombie--he might even be ready to go by the time you load up my steers."

"That's not what I wanted you to look at Ned. Take a look at that brand and tell me what you see."

The steer, realizing he wasn't going to get fed, turned his left side to them and walked towards the back side of the pen.

"Kinda haired over, but looks like a circle, cross and triangle to me. Why'd you ask?"

"Take a good look, Ned. Don't that remind you of something?"

Ned stepped down from the pen and walked slowly around the steer where he could get a better look. Then it dawned on him what Abercrombie was getting at. "Well, I be damned," he said. "A man with a running iron could make a C Bar A into that brand without much trouble. Where did he come from?"

"Man by the name of Borne, Henry Borne, brought about eleven hundred head in from New Mexico--over by the Rabbit Ears he said."

"I'd like to buy him from you, Mr. Abercrombie," Ned said.

"What you need with him, Ned, you got over three thousand head of the critters you're trying to sell."

"I'd like to get Mr. Boxwell down at the slaughter house to butcher him and pull that hide off. If that is a Ceebara steer, the inside of that hide is going to show where the brand has been doctored."

"Take him, Ned. I thought there was certainly a resemblance to your brand, and that's the reason I insisted he not go out with the rest of the cattle. We need to know if the Circle, Cross, Triangle is a legitimate ranch or if we got rustlers feeding off your herd."

"What about this Borne feller, Mr. Abercrombie, is he still in town?"

"Don't think so. He and his crew liquored up for a few days and left some of their money with the saloon girls, then rode out, headed west. That must have been about four days ago."

It was plain to see, when the hide was pulled off, that the steer was carrying a C Bar A brand that had been altered with a running iron. The Ceebara brand had been burned deep, through the hide--the Circle Cross Triangle had been burned so shallow that no scar was present on the inside.

Although Ned searched in every saloon and whore's crib in Dodge, there was no sign of Dutch Henry or any of his band of rustlers.

However, the town was full of tough buffalo hunters who were competing with his cowboys for the affections of the saloon girls. And many of his crew were young, green cowboys, who's courage exceeded their good judgement when they had a few drinks under their belts. The first night in town, several of his cowboys, overly imbibed, were caught up in a brawl with an equal number of dirty buffalo hunters. Had it not been for the intervention of three hundred pound City Marshall Larry Deger, there is no doubt that the cowboys would have been mauled by the knife wielding buffalo hunters. As it was, they were locked in the calaboose to sober up until morning.

Ned decided the sooner he could get the boys out of town, the safer it would be. Striking a deal with Abercrombie for sale of the herd, he loaded his wagon with supplies, tied Big Red behind the wagon and headed south.

With a few dollars in their pockets, some of the cowboys opted to remain in the sin city, not realizing that the crib girls would soon have those dollars stashed in their stockings and the cowboys would be out on the street, flat broke.

"Pa," Cole said as they left the town behind, "I don't think I like Dodge City nearly as much as I thought I would. They ain't nothing there except all them saloons--I counted seventeen--and all them painted up ladies trying to get the cowboys money. And it stinks something awful, with all them buffalo hides stacked next to the railroad, and the pens full of cattle waiting to be shipped. I reckon as how I'll be glad to get back to the ranch."

Ned laughed and replied, "I just hope you feel the same way ten years from now, Son."

* * * * * * * *

The Dutch Henry gang rode west out of Dodge City for five miles before turning south, in order to fool anyone who might be observing their movement. Dutch had put out information that his ranch was west of Dodge City, "over in New Mexico Territory by the Rabbit Ears," and didn't want folks wondering why he was headed south to Hidetown.

With winter coming on and his pockets full of gold from the sale of the eleven hundred head of Ceebara cattle, he wanted to enjoy his newly acquired wealth where there were women, whiskey, warm fires--and no law. Hidetown fulfilled all those requirements.

He would rather have spent the coming winter in Dodge City, but he couldn't take the chance that someone might question the legitimacy of the Circle Cross Triangle ranch, and wonder why he wasn't on the ranch looking after his cattle. Besides, Dodge City now had a marshall, and even though it was still a wild and unruly town, that marshall might look unfavorably on horse thieves and cattle rustlers. A person could shoot a man in a saloon brawl and get fined ten dollars for disturbing the peace, but if he stole a horse or a cow, he would be hanged on main street without a trial.

Hidetown would offer a pleasurable haven until next spring when he and his gang would once again start putting together another herd for sale in Dodge City. Next year he would have better pickings, what with that new herd over in the Palo Duro, and the Bugbee herd north of the Canadian.

* * * * * * * *

The first cold front blew onto the *Llano Estacado* in October, with temperatures falling to twenty degrees and a sprinkling of snow covering the prairie grass. It also influenced buffalo hunters to head for the hide center on the Sweetwater Creek, to market their hides and hibernate until spring when once again they would hit the trail of the diminishing herds.

Some of the hunters, with their wagons only half full of hides, opted to remain on the prairies, pursuing the scattered shaggies--a decision they would live to regret, as the winter of '76 took vengeance on the white interlopers. With only their wagons as protection from the harsh weather, their mule teams froze to death and many of the hunters, left afoot with supplies gone, died a horrible death and became food for the scavenging wolf packs.

One of the first hunting parties to take the trail down off the *Llano* to Hidetown, was that of Billy Dixon and Bat Masterson. Their four wagons, two Conestogas drawn by a span of six mules each, with a smaller trailing wagon hooked to the rear, were loaded with some of the finest hides to be brought in all year. The hair was long and thick as a result of Mother Nature's anticipation of the rough winter which was to come. A cook wagon, designed after the style of the cattleman's chuck wagon, brought up the rear as the small caravan crossed the Sweetwater Creek and pulled into Hidetown.

Bat Masterson, setting his huge sorrel gelding, and Billy Dixon, riding a tall dappled gray stallion, led the group down Main Street to show off their trophies. They pulled to a stop in front of the Lady Gay Saloon, tied their mounts and the mules to the hitching rail, and walked noisily into the rough interior of the *watering hole*.

In answer to a question from Teddy, the bartender, Billy Dixon replied, "We found 'em west of the Palo Duro, up on Tierra Blanca Creek. Big herd, probably two-three thousand head. Weren't no other hunters around so we took our time and loaded our wagons. Got all these hides along a five mile strip of the creek. Afore we found them, we searched that area from the Canadian all the way to the Tierra Blanca without seeing one head."

Bat interrupted Billy, "Nothing but dry bones scattered over the prairie from last year's kills all the way from the Canadian. What few herds that are left have all gone south. One more year and buffler hunting is going to be history, boys."

Teddy refilled their glasses, wiped a puddle of the spilled whiskey from the bar, and said, "That's hard to believe, Bat. Just last year, I remember seeing herds so big they reached from one horizon to the other, three or four miles across, grazing north. Ain't no way you hunters could have killed that many."

"Just take a ride up on the plains, Teddy, and you'll change your mind," Dixon said. "You can't ride more'n a half mile until you come upon another killing ground, with bones covering the grass for two or three hundred yards. Those damned shaggies are so dumb, they'll mill around their dead until our guns get so hot we cain't shoot no more."

"That's right, Teddy," Bat said. "I remember it used to be that way all the way to the Arkansas. But we cleaned those herds out three years ago, and then we started taking them south of the Arkansas, then south of the Cimmaron, and now south of the Canadian. If you want hides next year, you may have to hunt all the way south to the Yellow House or the Double Mountains."

The other hunters, gathered around to hear Dixon and Masterson spin their tales, began to argue amongst themselves. Jess Ross, a small hunter, somewhat cleaner than the others gathered around the bar, spit a brown stream of tobacco juice accurately into the brass spittoon, and said, "I 'spect Bat might be right, boys. My wagons were only half loaded when I come in, and I damned neart wore my teams out searching that country just south of the Canadian. If it hadn't been for a small herd I struck over on the North Fork, I'd of come up without a hide to my name."

"Don't mean nothing," Ben Thomas, still wearing his dirty, blood-soaked buckskins, spoke up as he pushed his gray-streaked hair back away from his eyes. "Them shaggies always head south way afore the snows start to fly. I'll bet my poke they'll be coming back come spring. Sure, they's less of them now than there was three year ago, but I think Teddy's right--ain't no way we could have kilt them all."

A tall, clean shaven and well dressed gent, sitting at one of the rough tables playing cards, spoke up. It was apparent he wasn't a buffalo hunter. "I just returned from a trip to Fort Griffin, boys, and the soldiers told me they's still thousands of shaggies west of the fort. I scouted me out a place on the Double Mountain Fork of the Brazos and will be sending a wagon train of supplies down in early spring to set up a trading center. I'll be buying all the hides you can bring in."

One of the younger hunters spoke up. "You ain't aiming to close down your store here in Hidetown, are you Mr. Rath?"

"No, Chad. We'll still be buying hides and selling supplies here on the Sweetwater. I'm just trying to make it easier on the ones that hunt down South. With a Post on the Brazos, you won't have to haul your hides nearly as far."

"Sounds like a good idea, Charlie. But I ain't made up my mind if I want to keep chasing buffaler," Bat interjected as he emptied the glass of whiskey he held in his hand. "Me and Billy did right well on this hunt, but there's going to be more hunters and less buffaler next year. I may pull up stakes and head back to Dodge City. I got a couple of brothers up there tryin' to uphold the law--I may just join them."

That statement brought a loud guffaw from the crowd of hunters. "You upholding the law, Bat! Why, that's like trying to git a whore into church on Sunday. You ain't no more law-abiding than I am," Ben said.

"Suit yourself, Bat, but you've got all winter to think it over. You and Dixon are two of the best hunters in the country. I hope you'll change your mind. Meanwhile, why don't we go take a look at that load of hides you brought in. I've got a wagon train going out to Dodge City tomorrow and yours will just about top them off."

Bat and Billy followed Charlie Rath out the door of the Lady Gay and watched as Rath walked around their wagons, looking and poking at the hides.

"Best I've seen all year, boys. I'm saying they're worth five-fifty a hide."

"We was told that there's been a lot of hides brought five-fifty in the last thirty days, Charlie. If'n ours is the best you've seen all year, they should be worth at least six dollars a hide," Billy Dixon said.

"Could be, and then maybe not. I've got to haul them all the way to Dodge before I know. Tell you what, though, I'll stretch it to five-seventy-five, not a penny more," Rath said, smiling at the two hunters.

Billy looked at Bat--Bat nodded, and Billy stuck out his hand to Rath. "You've got yourself a deal, Charlie. We'll be taking it all in gold. We don't aim to starve out those pretty girls on Feather Bed Hill or shut down the saloons because we ain't got gold to pay for our whiskey--and it may be a long, cold winter before we get another payday."

Charlie Rath laughed, "Park them wagons over by my diggings and I'll get some boys to start counting them off. I just hope I brought along enough gold coin to pay for them."

* * * * * * * *

Dutch Henry had arrived in Hidetown two weeks before Bat and Billy brought in their hides. With his pockets full of money from the sale of the rustled Ceebara cattle, he made quick work of looking over all of the girls, an estimated five hundred had invaded the town, and picked the one called Lill, who was the prettiest of the lot, to be his bed-mate for the coming winter.

The only criteria that Lill required for her companionship was gold coin paid daily, and a bath and clean clothes for her suitor weekly. Dutch paid the gold coin willingly, but reluctantly agreed to the bath and clean clothes.

Everyone knew Dutch had taken the outlaw trail after Hidetown had become the hide trading center of the plains, but no one knew of the rustled Ceebara herd and the sale that had taken place in Dodge City. And even if they had known, there was no one in Hidetown, other than Bat and Billy, who would have been concerned one way or another. And Bat and Billy knew nothing of his cattle business.

They had been friends, and along with Colonel Cole, had

been caught at Adobe Walls with Dutch during the attack by Quanah's army of Comanches, Cheyennes and Kiowas. Consequently, as fall turned to winter in Hidetown, the three veterans of the Adobe Walls battle, spent the long hours visiting the numerous saloons of Hidetown,drinking, gambling,telling stories about their experiences--and dallying with the ladies.

Bat, with experience surveying for the AT and SF railroad, took a job as surveyor for the town site of Hidetown, and spent some of his time laying off streets and lots.

Molly Brennan, teenaged daughter of Bob Brennan who had a boot repair shop in the rear of the Lady Gay Saloon, was one of the prettiest girls in town, and all of the cowboys and buffalo hunters had their eyes on her. However, Corporal Melvin King of nearby Fort Elliot, decided she was his lady and passed the word that he would kill anyone who he caught 'messing' with *his girl*.

Molly despised King and would have nothing to do with him.

One man, a drifter, had already died at the hands of King because of Molly, before Bat came to town. It was apparent that Bat and Molly were drawn to each other, and, to King's chagrin, Bat became her suitor.

King came to town with blood in his eyes, swearing he was going to put an end to Bat Masterson, who was coming between him and Molly. He found them in the Lady Gay, and as he stepped through the swinging doors, he drew his pistol and fired. However, Molly had been watching the door, and the split second before King fired, she stepped between Bat and the corporal, and caught the slug in her chest.

The bullet passed completely through her and entered

Bats hip, shattering the bone. As he was falling, Bat pulled his Colt and fired, striking the gunman in the heart.

Molly died in his arms and was the first person to be buried in the new, official cemetery, in Hidetown.

The hip was slow to heal, and left Bat with a noticeable limp, requiring the use of a cane when he walked. The painful wound and the diminishing herds of buffalo, combined to help him with his decision to end his hide hunting career. With the coming of spring, he left Hidetown and joined his brother Ed in Dodge City, to take up a law enforcement career.

Billy Dixon put together another hide-hunting crew and headed south for one more year of chasing the shaggies.

Dutch Henry, with the coming of spring, said goodbye to Lill and rode out to the new settlement on the Canadian, Atascosa, to await the arrival of the Ceebara herd on the plains, and his lucrative career as rancher--using other people's cattle. He was unaware that Ned had discovered his activities, and was laying plans to put a stop to those activities.

* * * * * * * *

And a new industry had blossomed in Hidetown and Atascosa--*bone picking*.

As the buffalo herds disappeared, the lucrative freight business of hauling hides to the railroad came to a standstill. Rather than return to Dodge City empty, the supply wagons were loaded with dried buffalo bones, hauled back to the railroad and shipped back east to be made into buttons, knife handles, and ground into fertilizer.

Thus the need for bone pickers was born, and hundreds

of scavengers invaded the area and began gathering the bones of the vanishing buffalo herds.

The bone pickers, a sorry lot who had no moral scruples, only added to the lawlessness that pervaded the area. Many of them, soon tired of the tedious, back-breaking work of gathering bones, realized there was much more money to be made gathering cattle instead of gathering bones--and entered into the rustling business.

* * * * * * *

11

"Yeah, I know Borne. He was pinned down with me and those buffalo hunters at Adobe Walls back in '74," Jim said, in answer to Ned's question. "Good shot, but didn't appear to have much ambition to work at hide hunting. After the battle, he headed back to Dodge City and I heard later that he had taken the outlaw trail. Horse thieving and train robbing was what I heard, but never heard of him stealing cattle."

"Well, Mr. Abercrombie says that's the name of the gent he bought the herd from--so looks like he may have branched out into the rustling business," Ned said, as they rode along at the head of the herd. Ceebara cowboys were strung out along the side and to the rear of the huge herd as they moved through the cut in the caprock.

The cattle had been brought in from the Washita, Sweet-water, and Red River winter pastures, worked in the corrals at headquarters, and were now being pushed back onto the plains. Working the herd, it was plain to see that they were short a thousand head or more from last year's count.

"I've been thinking, Colonel. He was so successful in rustling our herd last year that he's apt to try it again this year. Now that we understand how and where he's operating, we need to try to catch him red-handed."

"You're right, Ned. Sounds like you've got a plan."

"Yes, Sir, I have. You ain't going to like it, and I know Kate's going to raise Cain when she hears about it, but I think it'll work," Ned replied. "The Kid told me before he left that if I ever needed a favor, just holler. Well, I'm thinking we should send word to him to meet me at Atascosa, and him and me will pretend to be running from the law and see if we can join up with that Borne outfit. They don't know me, so it should be easy to move in on them."

"That's the worst plan I ever heard of, Ned! I'm not about to let you put yourself in danger like that. Why, if something happened to you, Belle and Kate would never forgive me," Jim said. And though he didn't voice it, he was thinking that he would never forgive himself if he let something happen to Ned.

"I don't aim to let nothing happen to me, Colonel," Ned answered. "And it ain't no more dangerous than scouting and fighting Indians, or getting caught by them Yankees in Virginny when you lost your arm. Dang it, we face danger every day of our lives out here on the frontier, and I think I can take care of myself. And I've seen the Kid in action--he'll back me up. Besides, somebody's got to stop them, or they'll steal every head we've got!"

"Well, we're partners, Son, and you've got a right to make decisions the same as me. I'm agin it, but if you think you can pull it off, I'm not going to try to stop you."

Ned smiled, "Thanks, Colonel, now you're going to have to help me convince Kate."

"That may be impossible, Ned, but we're going to have to offer more than a plan for you and the Kid to take on a whole gang of rustlers by yourselves, if we expect to convince her."

"Yes, sir, Colonel. I've given it a lot of thought. Give me and Kid a couple of weeks to work our way into the gang, then send Miguel to Atascosa. Tell him to look up that Casimiro Romero feller, and stay with him until I contact him. When I feel like everything is set up, I'll contact Miguel, give him the plan and he can come back to the ranch, get you and the boys, and we'll make our move."

"While we wait for Billy to get the message, we need to deliver Quanah's cattle to Fort Sill. I had the boys cut back five hundred head of cows and ten bulls and leave them along the North Fork, south of headquarters," Jim said. "It's time Jim Bold Eagle returned home, so we'll drive that bunch down the river--ain't more'n a hundred miles--to Quanah's stomping grounds. That'll give the boy a little more experience herding cows.

* * * * * * * *

When Billy the Kid received the message in New Mexico Territory, he told Mr. Chisum that he needed to take a few weeks off to help a friend, and promised to be back before winter.

"I guess we can get along without you for awhile, Kid, if you promise to be back by fall. Me and John Tunstall are putting together a syndicate to try to capture some of those government cattle contracts for the army and Indian reservations. If we get them, we're going to need all the help we can get."

"I'll be back, sir."

Billy tied his bedroll and poke behind his saddle,

shoved his rifle into the saddle boot, and struck out for Atascosa.

Ned, having let his beard and hair grow, dressed in tattered denims and riding an unbranded grulla gelding, rode into Atascosa a few hours ahead of the Kid. He was sitting in a corner of the newly established adobe saloon owned by Jack Ryan, nursing a warm beer and listening to some of the conversation that was going on at the bar. No one paid much attention to the tramp cowboy sitting in the corner with his back to the wall.

"I understand that Major Littlefield is bringing a herd in and is going to start a ranch somewhere along the river east of Atascosa," a tall cowboy said to Ryan, who was wiping glasses behind the bar.

"So I hear," Ryan replied, setting the glass alongside others lined up under the mirror.

"Might as well," a large, bear of a man, dressed in dirty buckskins interjected. "This country has gone to hell as a hide country. Ain't enough buffaler left to keep my skinners busy. Guess I'll be heading south, tomorrow. Hear tell they's big herds down around the Double Mountains."

"Well, *Senor*," a Mexican with a large sombrero on his head and a brightly colored *serape* thrown across his shoulder, said, looking at the buffalo hunter, "My sheep will be glad to see you leave, but they don't want to see more *vacas* coming. Already we have the longhorns to the east and to the south, and the *vaqueros* have told us to keep our sheep away from their *vacas*. How can we keep them away if they make their ranch where we are living?"

Ryan spoke, "Casimiro, It looks like the cowboys are coming, no matter what we think. Lee and Reynolds, the freight haulers, have been scouting around since the Indians were pushed off the plains, and I heard them talking about bringing in a herd and putting down roots somewhere along the Canadian. I don't know if your sheep and their cows are going to be able to run together or not."

The Mexican shook his head in disgust. "Maybe I'll start hauling freight, if the freight haulers are going to put me out of the sheep business."

"One good thing about it," Henry Kimball, local blacksmith and the first Anglo settler to set roots in Atascosa, said as he downed a shot of Ryan's cheap whiskey, "maybe the ranchers will rid us of that gang of cutthroats that's holed up over at Robber's Roost. Every time they ride into town, someone either gets beat up or killed. Now that the stage line is planning on putting in a line from Fort Elliot to Atascosa, we don't need them shooting up the stage or robbing freight wagons."

Ned listened intently, it was the first reference he had heard of a place called Robber's Roost. If Dutch Henry was operating in the area, that's where he would probably be found.

All eyes at the bar turned to the door when they heard the approach of a lone horse, stop, and the rider dismount and tie it to the hitching rail. The rider could be heard slapping the dust from his trousers with his hat, then the jingle of his spurs as he walked slowly towards the saloon doorway.

Ned watched as Billy stepped through the doorway and looked around. Spying Ned in the corner, he walked slowly across the room, looking at each face at the bar as he passed. His two Colts were tied low on his legs, and it was plain to see that a gunman had just come into town.

"Howdy, Kid," Ned said, as Billy pulled a chair forward and sat at the table facing Ned.

Smiling, Billy, nodded and returned the greeting. They did not shake hands, as it would have indicated that they had not seen each other for awhile. Their story would be that they had been separated after a robbery on the trail to Hide-town, when guards from the mule train had pursued them across the prairie. The story would be for Dutch Henry's ben-efit.

Ned motioned for the bartender to bring another beer, and he and Billy, speaking quietly enough that the others in the room could not hear, discussed plans to infiltrate the gang of cattle rustlers.

Atascosa, in its infancy, had little to offer in the way of accommodations for travelers. Leaving the saloon, Ned and the Kid mounted their horses and rode a quarter of a mile south and stopped in the shade of a large cottonwood tree, next to the bank of the Canadian River. Other travelers had used the tree as a campsite and had left a fire pit surrounded by large rocks. Ned dismounted and tied the grulla to a nearby bush and removed his saddle, dragging it near the fire pit.

Billy did the same. They both opened saddlebags and took out leather hobbles and placed them on the fore feet of their horses, removed their bridles and allowed the horses to graze the lush grass next to the river bank. After only a few bites of the grass, both horses lay down and began to roll in the soft sand, relieving the itch of the salt-stained sweat which had formed beneath the saddles.

"I 'spect this place is good as any to wait for Dutch to show his face," Ned said. "There's plenty of drift wood for a fire, and smooth sand where we can throw our bedrolls. I've got a little coffee in my saddlebags and an old pot in that gunny sack tied to my saddle horn."

"No need in trying to cook anything," Kid said. "I noticed a 'dobe when I rode in that had a sign said 'Scottie's Restaurant.' I figure it'll beat anything you or I can stir up, and since this little outing is being paid for by the Ceebara Cattle Company, we might's well make use of that Mexican cook I saw standing in the doorway."

Ned laughed. "No one said anything about paying you for your help, I thought this was just a little something for old-times sake."

"Old-times is alright, old friend, but it don't put beans on the plate. And I intend to eat well--after all, you never know when a meal is going to be your last when you're messing around with a band of cutthroats like Dutch Henry's gang," Billy joked.

Opening the other side of his saddlebags, Ned pulled out a leather pouch, filled with gold coins. Taking half of them, he handed them to Billy, and said, "Since you don't aim to help me as a friend, I guess you better stick these in your pocket--that makes me the boss! We was supposed to have robbed a freight wagon, so you need to have some gold to flash around."

Billy smiled, took the coins and looked at them before shoving them into his pocket. "Must be three or four hundred dollars --we must be pretty good highwaymen!"

"That's what I hope Dutch is going to think when we join up with him."

* * * * * * * *

After a meal of enchiladas and frijoles at Scottie's, Ned and the Kid returned to Ryan's Saloon. Dusk had fallen and the dim light of the coal oil lamps in the saloon reflected off the faces of a mixture of individuals--a few drifting cowboys, several buffalo hunters and even more Mexican sheepherders.

Ned noticed that Kimball was back, talking to a businessman named Howard, who apparently owned a new mercantile which he had just opened. Calling it a mercantile might have been stretching the point. Actually it was a small adobe structure with a few staples of food, medicines, firearms and whiskey--mostly whiskey.

"The first stage from Hidetown should arrive some time this week," Kimball told Howard, who was a newcomer to town. "That's going to really put us on the map. With the Indians all corralled back on the reservation, this country is going to boom--and we're setting in the best location on the plains. We've got the best crossing on the river, and the stage line is going to come right through here and then go on to Las Vegas. They're even talking about a stage line from Dodge City coming in pretty soon."

Howard held his drink up and smiling, said, "A toast--to Atascosa, an oasis with a future."

Kimball touched his glass to Howard's and they swallowed the contents, laughing at the thoughts of a few 'dobe buildings becoming the metropolis of the plains.

Ned and Billy listened with interest. Any news of the area could be used by them in their plans to infiltrate the gang of rustlers.

Two or three card games had begun between the cowboys and buffalo hunters. Others were standing around the bar, drinking and discussing buffalo, cattle and women, when the swinging doors flew open and a group of four, rough looking cowboys walked in, pushed their way to the bar and ordered the best whiskey in the house.   Ryan, reaching under the counter, pulled out a bottle of fine, imported whiskey and set it on the bar in front of the huge leader of the group.

"That's the best in the house, Mr. Henry," he said, as he pulled four glasses from the rack and pushed them towards the cowboys.

"How much for the bottle?" Dutch growled, as he pulled the cork with his teeth and started pouring the four glasses full.

"Five dollars."

"Highway robbery!" Dutch bellowed, as he tossed a five dollar gold piece onto the bar.

Not to be intimidated, Ryan responded, "What you expect- -that bottle came all the way from Scotland. If you want something cheaper, I've got it--made by a Cheyenne squaw about a mile down river. She ferments buffalo dung in mule piss and sells it for two-bits a bottle."

The other cowboys laughed, as they picked up their drinks and turned to search for a table in the crowded room.

Dutch led the way, carrying the bottle, and stopped before the table occupied by Ned and Billy.

"Looks like you two is setting at my table," Dutch said, "I 'spect you better move."

Ned sensed the Kid's body go tight, and reached his left hand out and placed it on the Kid's right arm, as if to say, "not now."

"I reckon as how you must be mistaken, mister. We been setting here for the past hour," he said, with his hands hid below the table and looking squarely into the dark, mean eyes of the intruder.

"I always set at this table when I come to town, everybody knows it," Dutch snarled.

As his hand dropped towards his gun, Ned said, quietly, "I wouldn't advise that, mister, I got a Colt pointed straight at your belly button, and my pardner has another one pointed at your friends. Now we don't want no trouble, and you're welcome to join us at *our* table--in fact, I'd be right glad to buy you a drink. See, I heard the barkeep call you Dutch, and we been looking for a feller named Dutch. Could be we might have some things in common, and no use in us seeing who can blow the biggest hole in the other until we talk about it a mite."

"Boss, maybe you should listen to what he says," one of the cowboys at his side said. Looking at Billy, and with a nervous twitch at the corner of his mouth, continued, "I remember seeing that Kid gun down four drifters who pulled down on him over some horses in Hidetown about a year ago!"

Dutch, moving his eyes from Ned to Billy, nervously hitched his thumb in his gun belt, set the bottle of whiskey down on the table, and said, "Jess, you and Tom find another table. Me and Tinker's going to set with these two and find out what makes them think they're so tough. Tinker, pull them two chairs over here."

Setting down, Dutch said, "You can put them guns back in your belt. If you're what I think you are, we may be able to work a deal."

"We won't have to put our guns up," Ned said as he placed his hands on the table. "We never had them drawn in the first place."

Dutch blinked, stared at Ned, then smiled. "You mean you was bluffing?"

Very calmly, Ned replied, "No, sir. We wasn't bluffing. If you'd gone for your gun, all four of you would be laying on the floor, messing it all up with your blood."

"Sound pretty sure of yourself, mister. What's your name?"

"Name's not important--but you can call me Reb--this here's my pardner, Kid."

"So why you looking for someone named Dutch?"

"Well, we heard that this Dutch feller was involved in a business which wasn't too well accepted by the law or the ranchers, and we thought he might need the help of a couple of like-minded citizens who are pretty good with a gun, a rope and a running iron."

"What makes you think I need someone like you? I've been doing just fine without you."

"Sure, you're doing fine--but what happens if things don't go just right and the law comes down on you--or even worse, if the ranchers discover what's happening to their cattle? You got enough wranglers that can shoot worth a damn in a tight?"

"Well, I can always use a good gun handler--but how do I know you don't just talk a good story?"

The kid spoke up, "You heard what Tom said about that shoot-out in Hidetown. But if that don't satisfy you, come down to our camp by the river in the morning and we'll give you a demonstration."

"O.K., Kid, I'll do that, and if you can handle a gun the way you claim, I'll take you on."

* * * * * * * *

Next morning, Ned and Billy were sitting on their bed-rolls next to the fire, drinking coffee, when Dutch and Tinker rode up. They dismounted and dropped their reins. The horses sneezed, shook their bodies then dropped their heads and started nibbling at the grass next to the river. Ned's and the Kid's horses, still hobbled, looked them over, and, unconcerned, dropped their heads and continued to graze.

"So you think you're pretty good with a gun," Dutch said as Ned stood, and faced him squarely. "Folks say I'm the best," he added, and with no warning, shouted, "Draw!"

His hand dropped towards his Colt, but before he even started to pull it from its holster, he was staring at the end of Ned's pistol, pointed at his heart.

"Well, I be damned!" he said, moving his hand back above his belt. "You are good!"

"Not as good as Kid," Ned said. "He could have put two holes in your shirt pocket before you broke leather."

"O.K., Reb, you've made your point. You can draw but can you shoot?

"See that rock out in the middle of the river? Probably fifty feet. Kid--show the man what happens to folks that draw on you," Ned said.

No sooner had he finished the sentence than the Kid's Colt was in his hand, smoking, and the rock exploded into hundreds of pieces. One of the larger pieces flew straight up. With lightning speed, Ned drew and fired. The piece shattered in mid-air.

Dutch had seen enough.

"I'm just now putting together my gang. You two boys will

make fine additions. Here's the rules--I get half of every thing we take in, the rest is divided equally between you and the others. In addition, I'll pay you cowhand wages until we get our herd gathered and sold. Just remember, I'm the boss--you'll do what I say!"

"How many we have to share with?" Billy asked.

"Right now there's only the three you saw last night, a cook and two more wranglers back at camp. If we need more, I'll hire them, but the nine of us should be able to handle it," the outlaw answered.

"Fair enough," Ned said. "Where you want us to park our poke?"

"About five miles upriver, there's a canyon comes into the river from the south, with running water. It's hard to see, but you'll find a large boulder next to the river bed and a crooked cedar tree growing next to it. There's a small stream flowing between the rock and cedar. The canyon widens out after you leave the river. Follow the stream for a couple of miles and you'll come to our diggings in a cottonwood grove. Ain't much, a couple of rock houses that the sheep herders abandoned and a few hide tents to keep us out of the weather. Good grazing for a small herd, and just a few miles over to New Mexico Territory. There's a little trading post a few miles further west called Trujillo, on the trail to Las Vegas. We're far enough off the trail that no one is going to be bothering us while we put together our herd," Dutch explained.

* * * * * * * *

The Ceebara cattle had been left to themselves for the

159

summer in the west pasture, and the cowboys had returned to headquarters to build additional working pens. Keeping all the female calves, the herd was now growing at the rate of ten thousand a year, and it kept the crew of over fifty cowboys busy during the summer preparing for the fall roundup. With no permanent water on the *Llano Estacado,* Colonel Cole had not yet decided to build pens on the plains. He and Ned had discussed plans for a ranch house and additional gathering area on the Canadian River just south of Adobe Walls, but that would not be started until next year.

As usual, some of the cattle had continued to graze westward, and had strayed off the Ceebara range. Some of them, over five hundred head, had even strayed to a large playa lake nearly due south of Atascosa.

Dutch Henry and his gang would have little problems gathering a herd from the thousands of longhorns which had strayed off the Ceebara Ranch. Dutch had noticed another smaller herd which was now grazing across the river to the north, carrying the Quarter Circle T brand. It wasn't as large a herd, but there were a lot of calves which had not yet been branded.

It was probably time for him to start thinking of building a legitimate ranch, and a few unbranded calves taken from north of the river would be a good place to start.

"Tinker, I want you to ride out ahead of the rest of us. Once you get into the grazing herd, ride on east at least five miles. Mosey around and keep a sharp eye out. If you see any of the Ceebara crew heading our way, hightail it back and sound the alarm. We'll quit what we're doing and ride back into Atascosa," Dutch ordered.

"Sure, Boss," Tinker answered. "How long you want me

to stay out."

"Give us about four hours, then come on back. We'll try to cut out a hundred head of the first ones we come across and head 'em west. We'll keep well south of the river until after we pass Atascosa, then we'll drop off into our canyon. If we push them hard, we should have them safe by dark."

Ned, the Kid and the other two cowboys joined Dutch and rode out of the canyon to the flat prairies on top. Riding east, they skirted several smaller canyons before making contact with the first longhorns. The warm weather had caused the cattle to shed most of their winter hair, and the C Bar A brand could be seen plainly on the left hip. Most of the calves were six weeks to two months old and were carrying no brand at all.

Dutch decided that this year he would keep the calves with the cows, and use them as a foundation herd for his legitimate ranch.

Riding through the scattered grazing herd, they counted out a hundred head of cows and steers, and headed them west. At first the cattle didn't want to leave the main herd, but soon realized that it was hopeless to resist the cowboys. Soon they were moving at a brisk pace towards their new home at Robber's Roost, with cowboys on either side and two pushing from the rear.

After four hours, Dutch ordered the crew to stop and allow the cattle to rest. Some of the younger calves were beginning to fall back and slow the herd. While they were resting, Tinker caught up with the herd and reported that all was clear to the rear. "Haven't seen hide nor hair of anybody since I left you this morning," he said.

With Tinker to help, the herd was pushed harder, and before the sun dipped below the horizon in the west, they dropped off the prairie into their hidden canyon and allowed the cattle to drink in the small stream.

* * * * * * * *

"I'm worried, Colonel," Kate said, as they were having breakfast. "Ned's been gone a week and we haven't heard a thing about where he is or what he's doing. We don't even know if Billy met him in Atascosa."

"Now, don't fret, Kate. No news is good news. If things were not going right, Ned would let us know."

"We can't be certain, Colonel. What if he's hurt, or if the rustlers found him out and have him locked up somewhere. I think we should go ahead and send Miguel. At least he would be close by to help if Ned needs him."

"If it'll make you feel any easier, we'll send him. That can't do any harm. We just don't want to do anything that might compromise Ned's plans."

Jim pushed his chair back and stood up, put on his hat and walked to the bunkhouse. Calling Miguel outside, he instructed him to prepare to go to Atascosa. "Better take along a packhorse and plenty of supplies to last awhile. You never can tell what you might run into or what Ned may need. Don't try to make contact with Ned--he'll reach you when he's ready. Just tell Romero that you need to stay with him for a few days. When Ned contacts you, you get the message to me in a hurry.

Placing his arm around Miguel's shoulders, he said, "O.K., boy, get started!"

* * * * * * * *

The next day after bringing the first hundred head of cattle into the valley of Robber's Roost, the rustlers began the job of changing brands. Ned and Kid were given the task of heading and heeling the older cows, dragging them to the fire, and holding them until Dutch doctored the brand to make the C Bar A into a Circle Cross Triangle. Tinker, with a sharp pocket knife, changed the ear-mark so that no one would recognize it as being a Ceebara mark. The other two cowboys, kept the fire going and the running irons hot.

By nightfall, a hundred head of Ceebara cattle had become Circle Cross Triangle cattle and Dutch was ready to make a second sortie out on the plains to round up another hundred head.

"Dag nab it, boss," Tom said when Dutch announced his plans for another drive, "we got all summer, why don't we take a day off and ride into Atascosa and wet our whistles. Them buffalo hunters are going to drink it dry and won't leave us anything but creek water!'

"I guess one day ain't going to hurt," Dutch replied. "O.K., boys, we'll ride in tomorrow for a little rest and relaxation."

That was going to simplify Ned's plans. While Dutch and the others were celebrating, he planned to slip away and contact Miguel. With a hundred head of Ceebara cattle rustled and another hundred on the way, he had plenty of evidence to hang Dutch and his gang.

Jack Ryan's Saloon was doing a booming business. The first stage had arrived from Hidetown with mail and a load of passengers, mostly *painted* ladies from Feather Bed Hill in Hidetown who were looking for new territory to conquer.

163

Atascosa was now on the map, as Ryan had predicted.

Dutch, Ned, Kid, and the other cowboys rode into town as the stage was unloading. After eyeballing the ladies, they walked into the saloon and shoved their way up to the bar. Ned quickly downed a beer and told Dutch he believed he would look around town for awhile.

"Going to find out where them pretty ladies are bedding down, 'eh?" Dutch asked.

Smiling, Ned only nodded his head, turned and walked away. Without hurrying, he walked down the dirt street, looking unconcerned at the crowd around the stagecoach, turned the corner, then walked briskly towards the Romero compound.

Stepping to the door, he knocked and removed his hat when a lovely, dark eyed senorita greeted him.

"*Buenos Dias, senor*," she said, "*Como sta?*"

"*Buenos Dias, senorita, hablar Engles?*" Ned replied in broken Spanish.

"*Si, senor, un poko*," she said. "A little."

"I am looking for my friend, Miguel Garcia, from the Ceebara ranch."

"Come in, *senor*. He is talking with my father on the plaza."

Ned followed her to the rear of the adobe where Miguel and Casimiro Romero were seated under the shade of a huge cottonwood tree, sipping tequila.

"Papa, this *vaquero* wishes to speak to *senor* Garcia," she said, as Casimiro rose to shake Ned's hand.

"Ned Armstrong, *senor*," Miguel said in introduction.

Ned flinched when Miguel introduced him by his real name. The Mexican cowboy smiled and said, "Don't worry,

Ned. *senor* Romero is a friend. I have told him about the rustlers and how you are trying to put an end to it. He wishes to
help in any way that he can. He says that the outlaws from
Robber's Roost are a plague on the area and he wishes to see
them hung to the nearest tree."

Romero spoke up, "*Si, senor*, I will keep your secret. In
the past month, the *pistoleros* from Robber's Roost have
killed two of my herders, for no reason at all. I am afraid to
even allow my wife and daughter to walk the streets of Atascosa because of what they have done to other women in our
town."

"Thank you, *senor* Romero," Ned said, "You have been a
big help by allowing Miguel to stay in your *Casa* until I came.
I may ask for more help, later. But for now, things are going
as planned."

Turning to Miguel, Ned instructed, "Hightail it back to the
ranch, Miguel, and tell the Colonel to bring a couple of the
cowboys and meet me here at *senor* Romero's *casa*," looking to Romero for agreement.

Casimiro nodded his permission.

"I will contact him, here, probably in about three or four
days."

"*Bueno*," Miguel nodded as he stood and walked towards
the stable. Piedad, Casimiro's daughter, followed at his side.
She looped her arm in his and looked affectionately at his
face as he stopped at the door of the stable.

"You must be careful, Miguel," she said, concerned. "I
will be waiting for your return."

Miguel squeezed her hand and nodded without replying.
He had always been uncomfortable around girls, but this one
had stolen his heart.

Ned smiled and thought, *So, friend, it looks as if we soon will have another wedding at the Ceebara Ranch.*

* * * * * * * *

It was a hard ride, from Atascosa to Ceebara headquarters. But Miguel made it by midnight, riding first his cowhorse, then switching to the packhorse which he had trailed behind. Both horses were winded and covered with sweat when he rode into the ranch compound.

Shep welcomed him back with an excited bark, as he rushed up the steps of the veranda and banged on the ranch house door.

"Colonel!" he shouted, "It's me, Miguel. Open the door!"

Sleepy-eyed, Jim opened the door, wearing only his long johns and holding a coal oil lamp in his hands. "What is it, boy? Has something happened to Ned?"

"No, sir, but Ned says you need to get to Atascosa as soon as possible. He thinks that things will be ready for a showdown in three or four days."

"Come in, son. There's cold beans and steak on the stove. Grab you a bite while I get dressed," he said as he stepped towards the bedroom.

Belle, pulling her robe around her, stepped into the kitchen, followed close behind by Kate.

"I'll have the coffee ready, soon," she said as she stoked the still glowing ashes in the stove.

"Ned! what about Ned?" Kate asked, fear plainly showing on her face.

"Ned's fine, Miss Kate," Miguel mumbled with his mouth full of beans. "Don't you worry none. Ned's fine! He and the

Kid got in with the rustlers, and they've already rounded up a hundred head of our cattle and placed a Circle Cross Triangle brand on them. He says they will be going back after another bunch tomorrow, and he thinks we can catch them in the act of burning brands on them the next day."

Jim stepped into the kitchen, buckling his gunbelt around his waist. "I'll wake Slim and Sonny and take them with me," he said. "You get them clothes off and get some sleep, boy, you've had a hard day."

"No, sir!" Miguel replied, "I'm fine. I'm going with you. Ned might need me--I'm going!" He didn't say, but the thoughts of Piedad waiting for him in Atascosa was also reason for him to go.

He said it with such finality, that Jim figured there was no need to argue. "O.K., you can go, but you go in there and lay down on my bed and rest while I get things together and get the boys up."

Turning to Belle, he said, "Better rustle us up some grub to take along, Kate. Something we can chew on while we're riding."

* * * * * * * *

The arrival of the new girls to Atascosa on the stage had changed Dutch's plans. Jack Ryan had wasted no time in hiring them to entertain in his saloon, and the small frontier town had bounced with the sound of celebration coming from the small adobe structure until well after midnight.

As usual, Dutch staked his claim on the prettiest of the lot, a red head named Squirrel, and when a hide skinner questioned his right to the girl, a brawl ended with the skinner rushing from the saloon, holding a bleeding arm. Dutch replaced the long-bladed knife in the scabbard on his belt, grabbed Squirrel by the arm and pulled her to his table. When the celebration ended, he accompanied her to a small adobe at the rear of the saloon where she had set up residence. The sun had moved well past midday before he awoke, and the pleasures of the night had convinced him that another day's wait before resuming his rustling business would be worthwhile. Besides, he had no idea where the other members of his gang had holed up--probably with other members of the newly arrived female entertainers.

Ned and Kid had slipped away before midnight and rode to the Romero plaza. Romero welcomed them and offered them lodging for the night. The next morning, while sharing breakfast at Romero's table, Ned discussed his plans with his host.

"*Senor* Romero, Colonel Cole should arrive from the ranch today or tomorrow. It's apparent that Dutch and the other rustlers will be in no condition to continue their work today, so I may still be in town when the Colonel arrives. Kid and I will need to hang around Ryan's saloon until we receive orders from Dutch. I'd appreciate it if you would look me up when the Colonel arrives."

"It will be my pleasure, Ned," Casimiro replied.

Returning to the saloon by mid-morning, Ned and Kid chose a table next to the wall, and passed the time playing cards until Dutch showed up, looking like a horse that had been rode hard and put up wet.

Not bothering to explain where he had been, Dutch said, "Too late to do anything today. I guess I'll stay over another night here in Atascosa. You boys do whatever you like, I'll meet you at the camp in the morning and we'll make another drag across the plains tomorrow."

He turned, walked out the door and crossed the street to Scottie's Restaurant.

He had been gone only a short time when Casimiro Romero entered the saloon and walked up to the bar. By now there were several customers lining the bar, nursing their drinks and discussing the prospects of Atascosa growing, since it was now a stop on the stage line from Fort Elliot to Las Vegas.

Glancing at Ned, Casimiro nodded and then looked out the door. Ned and Billy picked up their cards and walked outside. They pretended to adjust the saddles on their horses which were tied to the hitching rail, until Romero stepped from the saloon. Once again he nodded and walked down the street towards his plaza.

Ned and Billy mounted their horses, rode west a short distance before turning north, then back east to Romero's house. Riding to the rear, they quickly led their horses into the stable, where several more horses, wet with sweat and carrying the C Bar A brand were nibbling on hay.

Colonel Cole, Miguel, Slim and Sonny were seated at the huge dining table next to the kitchen, drinking coffee and talking to Romero when Ned and Billy entered the house.

"Howdy, Colonel," Ned said, smiling. "You're a sight for sore eyes."

"Got here soon as we could," Jim said. "Almost rode our horses into the ground, but we made good time."

Ned and Billy shook hands with the rest of the Ceebara crew, then accepted coffee from Casimiro.

"Everything's looking good, Colonel. We worked our way

into the gang with no problems, and we've already changed brands on a hundred head. Dutch has six more cowboys besides me and the Kid. It's a pretty tough bunch, but we shouldn't have any trouble taking them if you slip in while we're branding the next herd."

"When you think that will be?" Jim asked.

"The plans now are that we will make a drag across the plains tomorrow, and mark and brand them the next day. Dutch is so sure of himself, he hasn't been posting any guards in the canyon. I think if you and the boys would ride in about noon, the day after tomorrow, you should be able to catch us red-handed, with our running irons hot."

"Sounds good, Ned," Jim said. "Maybe you'd better draw us a map of the layout."

Casimiro gave Ned a sheet of paper and pencil and he drew a rough map of the canyon, where it intersected the Canadian River, and marked the approach to the holding pens.

"I'd leave your horses here, by this big rock in the stream bed. It's only about a quarter of a mile to the pens and you can stay pretty well out of sight if you walk in the creek. You'll come out of the creek, here," and he pointed to a mark immediately behind the corrals. "There's a half-dozen cedar trees that will hide you from their view. When you get in place, fire one shot in the air to alert me and Kid. We'll have our guns on them before they realize what is happening."

Casimiro spoke up. "*Senor* Cole, I will go with you. I know the canyon well, for I have grazed my sheep there. Maybe you will need a witness that they are stealing your *vacas*."

* * * * * * * *

The drive was made without problems, the cattle penned in the canyon, and the following morning, branding and marking began.

By noon, half of the herd had been branded and Ned and the Kid were dragging a large steer to the fire when a shot rang out. Releasing the dallys on their ropes, Ned and Kid turned their horses, facing Dutch and the other cowboys who were working around the branding fire. However, being out of position with the steer on their ropes, they were slow to get their guns drawn.

Dutch and the others had their guns out and were firing towards the cedars when Ned shouted for them to drop their weapons.

Dutch turned and fired before Ned could respond, hitting him in the shoulder and knocking him from his horse. Kid dropped to the ground behind his horse and fired, knocking Dutch's gun from his hand, and at the same time shouting for the others to drop their guns. When they failed to comply, and instead, turned their guns towards Ned, Kid took two of them down with quick shots.

Meanwhile, Jim and the Ceebara cowboys rushed from the protection of the cedars, spraying the corral with a withering fire, shouting for them to drop their guns. Two more of the rustlers fell, one holding his leg where blood was coloring his trousers, the other dead with a bullet in his chest.

Dutch, blood pouring from his bleeding hand, shouted for the remaining gunmen to drop their weapons, and held his hands in the air.

The battle was over in less than thirty seconds, with three rustlers dead, Dutch and one other wounded. Ned was sitting in the middle of the corral, holding his bleeding shoulder. Billy rushed to his side, "Damn it, Ned, I should have been faster. I let that sidewinder get off a shot before I could get him in my sights. I'm sorry!"

"Weren't your fault, Kid. If we wouldn't have had that steer on our ropes, it never would have happened. I don't think it's too bad. I can still move my arm and shoulder, must have gone clean through without hitting a bone."

Dutch, holding his bleeding hand, looked at Ned and Kid and cursed them, realizing that he had been duped.

Jim rushed up and knelt beside Ned. Removing his bandana from around his neck, he placed it over the bleeding hole. "Here, hold this in place until the bleeding stops, son," he said. "Miguel, look in my saddlebags and bring me that bottle of snake bite medicine. We'll pour a little of it on this hole and a lot of it down Ned's throat. That should keep him quiet for awhile."

Ned grimaced and said, "Trying to repay me for putting that hot blade to your arm to stop the blood back there on the battlefield in Virginny, Colonel?"

"Good whiskey beats a hot blade, anytime, son," Jim said affectionately.

* * * * * * * *

After burying the dead rustlers, they led Dutch and the remaining four cattle renegades to Atascosa, where Romero had an empty, windowless adobe building, which had been used as a tack room.

Many of the crib girls stood in the doorway of the saloon and watched as the Ceebara crew rode down the street with the rustlers in tow. One of the girls watching was Squirrel, who had shared Dutch Henry's bed. She watched with interest as the rustlers were locked in the makeshift jail.

Colonel Cole shoved Dutch and the other rustlers into the room, slammed the door and locked it. "We best keep a guard posted until we leave for the fort in the morning, Ned. Dutch may have friends who might try to bust him out."

"Dutch has no friends in Atascosa, Colonel, but no need to take any chances. I'll take first watch, Sonny can spell me at midnight, and Kid can take over at four," Ned responded.

At midnight, Sonny replaced Ned at the make-shift jail. "There's beans and steak on the table in Romero's kitchen, Ned, and he said to help yourself. Colonel and the others are bunking in the barn."

"Alright, Sonny. Keep alert, those are pretty rough hombres in there. They'd as soon slit your throat as to skin a shaggie. They know they are going to end up at the end of a rope, so they'll do anything to escape."

"Don't worry, Ned. I'll be careful."

Sonny could hear the music, the laughing and screaming coming from the nearby saloon. Once in awhile, the high pitched voice of an inebriated female could be heard, casting obscenities at some drunk cowhand. Sonny smiled, imagining at the celebration that was taking place only a few hundred yards away. The moon was shining brightly, and as the night wore on, couples soon started leaving the saloon, weaving towards the nearby cribs of the *painted ladies*.

Suddenly, from out of the dark, a lone lady appeared. It was apparent that she was very drunk by the way she walked. As she came near, she stumbled and fell into Sonny's arms.

Sonny held her to keep her from falling, and guided her

173

to the bench in front of the adobe building.

"Thanks, cowboy," she slurred. "Guess I had one too many."

"Looks that way, Miss," Sonny said, smiling. "You'd best set awhile."

In the moonlight, he could see that she was a very pretty lady, long red hair that fell around her shoulders and soft lips that sparkled with moisture when she talked. Her dress was rumpled, and one side had fallen from her shoulder, revealing the soft, white skin below her neck and above her partly exposed breast.

"Maybe you and me could have a party," she said, looking at Sonny, coyly.

When she weaved forward and it appeared she would fall from the bench, Sonny leaned towards her to push her back against the wall. He never saw her right arm swing up, her hand holding a pistol by its barrel, as it struck him with force on his temple.

He crumpled in a heap at her feet. She immediately swung the pistol again and hit him hard in the back of the head. The world went dark, and Sonny was unaware of her pushing him away from the door then releasing the latch and whispering, "Come on Dutch, honey--it's me, Squirrel. I've got horses tied out back."

The rustlers rushed from the tack room and followed her to the horses, which were saddled and ready to ride.

Dutch turned the horses down the street and headed west, towards the New Mexico border.

* * * * * * * *

174

"I'm sorry, Colonel," Sonny said, holding the back of his head. "This drunk lady staggered up to the cell and fell. I caught her and set her on the bench, and that's the last I remember."

When Billy had come to take over guard duty, he found Sonny still crumpled where Squirrel had left him, the door was open and the adobe was empty. He tried to awaken Sonny, but when he was unsuccessful, he rushed back to the Romero plaza and awakened Jim.

"Don't fret, son, I'd have done the same thing. There was no way you could tell that she was pretending to be drunk so she could take you unawares," Jim said after they had carried Sonny to the barn, poured water on his face and awakened him.

"Could you tell which way they went, Colonel?" Sonny asked, grimacing at the pain in his head.

"Afraid not, Sonny. Too many tracks in the street, and there was no way to determine which was their's."

"We better get our horses saddled and see if we can find them, Colonel," Miguel said.

"It'd be a waste of time, boy. Besides, Ned and Sonny are not fit to ride. We need to get them back to the Doc at Fort Elliot. Now that Dutch and his renegades know that we're on to their tricks, I don't think they'll be bothering Ceebara cattle for awhile."

Slim interrupted, "Colonel, you won't be needing me and Miguel. We'll ride back to their camp, gather our cattle and head them back to the ranch while you take Ned and Sonny back to the fort."

"Alright, Slim, but be careful, there's a chance that Dutch may have returned to the cattle," Jim cautioned.

Casimiro Romero had joined them in the barn and was listening to the conversation. "*Senor* Cole, you can take my buckboard and team. *Senor* Ned does not need to be riding a horse. I will send Frank along with you and he can bring the rig back."

"Thank you, *Senor* Romero," Jim replied, "That will be good."

Kid spoke, "Ned, I'll help Slim and Miguel with the cattle, then I'm heading back to Mr. Chisum's ranch. I promised him I'd only be gone two or three weeks."

"Thanks, Kid," Ned replied, "I owe you a lot, and I won't forget."

"You owe me nothing, Ned. That's just small payment for you standing with me at Hidetown."

12

The spring of 1878 was seeing many changes in the Texas Panhandle. The stage line between Hidetown, Atascosa, and Las Vegas began delivering mail, and the names of the Panhandle's first two towns had to be changed. Hidetown became Sweetwater, and when it was discovered that there was already a Sweetwater in Texas, the town leaders asked some Indian scouts at the fort for the Indian name for sweet water. Mobeetie was the name given, but some say the Indians played a trick on the buffalo hunters and that Mo-bee-tee actually is translated as buffalo dung.

Since there was also an Atascosa, Texas, on the mail rolls, the *A* was dropped from the spelling and Atascosa became Tascosa.

John Adair had joined Charles Goodnight as a partner in the cattle business, with a ranch in Palo Duro Canyon. The brand was changed, and the Goodnight ranch would henceforth be known as the JA.

Bugbee's Quarter Circle T was prospering north of the Canadian, and he had extended his grazing lands to the north and west.

Mobeetie and Tascosa remained the only two towns in

the Texas Panhandle until the Reverend L.H. Carhart started a colony on the Salt Fork of the Red River for his followers of the Methodist persuasion, just fifty miles southwest of Mobeetie. The town was named Clarendon, after his wife, Clara. It also was understood there would be no saloons or brothels in the town, consequently, the cowboys and buffalo hunters were quick to nickname it *Saint's Roost,* a name that would keep the rough and rowdy from putting down roots in the town proper.

The Reverend Carhart, realizing the land was not only a good place to start a Christian colony, also recognized it was great cattle country. With the help of his brother-in-law's financing, he staked off 343 sections of grass north of Goodnight's JA ranch, bought cattle and started the Half-Circle Heart ranch.

As Saint's Roost grew with teetotaling Christians, Mobeetie grew with sinners. The number of saloons swelled to thirteen, and the number of prostitutes to five hundred. An entire city block was devoted to living quarters for the *painted ladies*, and was referred to as *Feather Bed Hill.* The ladies were not lacking in customers with over five hundred woman-hungry soldiers stationed at Fort Elliot, hundreds of buffalo hunters bringing in their hides, mule-skinners from the numerous wagon trains, gamblers and gunmen by the dozens, and now, cowboys looking for a place to spend their hard-earned salaries, and whoop it up for awhile.

And the number of law-enforcing officers remained at zero. However, there was none needed, since there were *no* laws to be broken. Anything was legal in Mobeetie.

Cattlemen, learning of the free grass began trailing herds into the Panhandle from South Texas, New Mexico, Colorado and Kansas. By year's end, Major George Littlefield had established his LIT brand on the Canadian--Lee and Scott, the LS just east of Tascosa--Reynolds, the LE west of Tascosa--Bates and Beal, the LX north of the Canadian--and McAnulty, the Turkey Track, east of Adobe Walls.

The Texas Panhandle, an eight million acre tableland of free grass had become the cattle grazing capital of the world!

Eight million acres of uncharted, unsurveyed grassland-- with no law, and essentially no government. A land where the lawless were pulled, as if by a vacuum.

A land where strong-willed men must make and enforce their own laws.

* * * * * * * *

"This country is getting too damned populated," Jim said as he and Ned were riding the west pasture.They had left ranch headquarters the day before, trailing a packhorse loaded with enough supplies to last a week. "All kinds of strange brands are showing up. Look there, that's a LX brand on that steer, and that one over there is carrying a Quarter Circle T. Before the year is out we're going to have cattle from every dad-blasted brand in the Panhandle grazing our grass!"

"That's for danged sure, Colonel," Ned replied. "There's a couple of Turkey Track cows with that bunch. And last week, I was riding the north pasture and came onto a couple hundred Quarter Circle T cows grazing with our cows south of the river. Ain't no way we can keep 'em separated."

"I 'spect it's time to put some organization into this situation," Jim said. "When we get back to headquarters, I'll send some of the boys to the other ranches and invite them over for a conflab."

"What you think we can do about it, Colonel?"

"I guess the first thing we need to do is get acquainted with our neighbors, and see what kind of people we are competing with. We need to make certain they don't start putting their brands on our calves."

"Why don't me and you ride over to the Big Canyon and see Colonel Goodnight. He said he'd like to meet you, and this might be a good time for you to make his acquaintance."

"That's as good a place to begin as any, I suppose. Goodnight is probably having the same problems, what with that new Carhart ranch setting up headquarters just a stone's throw from his north line. And I understand there's a new outfit taking shape just south of his ranch called the Matador."

"We told Belle and Kate we'd probably be gone a week, why don't we ride over to the Big Canyon and make a visit with Colonel Goodnight," Ned said, "his headquarters is no more than a day's ride from here."

"Good idea, Ned," Jim replied.

They turned their mounts to the south and rode towards the Palo Duro Canyon, all the while watching for strange brands on the grazing longhorns which dotted the prairie.

Reaching the rim of the canyon just before sundown, the two cowboys sat their horses and watched with awe as the huge chasm cut in the prairie's floor changed colors a hundred times as the sun's rays were blocked out by the canyon's rim.

"I never cease to be thrilled at that sight, Ned. I remember the first time Belle and I laid eyes on it back in sixty-six. We came up from the east side, just about this time of day, and was on the rim before we realized that the canyon existed. It looked as if a huge slice had been cut out of the prairie, without disrupting the terrain on either side. I can tell you, it took our breath away. It is simply unbelievable!"

"Yes, sir, Colonel, it affects me the same way. My Ma would say it would take the hand of God to create something like this."

"And she'd be right. How far to the trail that leads down to Goodnight's headquarters, Ned?"

"Another couple of hours ride, Colonel. We best make camp here, and ride down in the morning."

A small fire of buffalo chips was soon glowing as they made coffee and warmed beans and bacon for the evening meal. The horses and pack mule were hobbled and allowed to graze on the thick mat of gramma grass along the canyon's rim.

Rolling out their bedrolls next to the fire, they lay looking at the millions of stars which dotted the darkened sky, seeing the bright tails of numerous meteorites which burned up their lives as they plunged into the earth's atmosphere.

Then, as if by magic, the darkness began to glow--first, with a faint lightening of the sky, then a burst of orange as the outlines of a full moon began to rise across the black depths of the great canyon.

Both men arose from their bedrolls without a word, and stood looking with awe as the moon's rays lit up the floor of the canyon. The two horses and the mule, as if on cue, stopped their grazing and silently looked with the men, towards the rising moon.

They were in the saddle by sunup and, finding the faint Indian trail along the canyon's walls, began their descent to the floor of the canyon. A small plume of smoke, no more than a mile down the small stream, rose silently into the still air of the morning, announcing the presence of Goodnight's headquarters.

Like most early plains homesteads, the headquarters was merely a half-dugout, with rafters made from lodge poles, which had been found in an abandoned Comanche campground nearby. The lodge poles were covered with sod to protect the inhabitants from the infrequent rains which fell in the canyon. Close by, the skeletal form of an uncompleted log cabin could be seen.

As Jim and Ned rode up, Hard Tack, the cook, stepped from the door of the dugout and threw a pan of dishwater into the yard.

"Well, bless my bones, if it ain't Ned Armstrong," he shouted. "Colonel Goodnight, come out here and look. We got company!"

The big, raw-boned frame of Charles Goodnight, stepped out the door and walked towards the two riders. A lovely lady stood in the doorway and watched as the riders dismounted.

"Ned," he said, "light down off that horse and shake my hand! I been wondering how you folks was getting along."

"We been doing right well, Colonel," Ned replied. "I'd like for you to meet my friend, Colonel Jim Cole."

Goodnight reached out and took Jim's left hand in his right, and shook it , paying no attention to the empty sleeve. "Seems like I already know you, Colonel, what with all the stories Ned told about you."

Jim smiled, "I hope they weren't all lies, Colonel. Glad to meet you."

"Seems you and me are carrying the same moniker, Colonel," Goodnight said, smiling. "It'd suit me just fine if you called me Charlie."

Jim laughed, "Might keep down some confusion. I'll call you Charlie if you'll call me Jim."

"Alright, Jim. You and Ned come in. This diggins ain't much, but it's got a good fire and a coffee pot that stays hot all the time. Hard Tack, pour our neighbors some coffee!"

"Jim, I'd like for you to meet my wife, Molly--and Molly, meet Ned Armstrong. This is the young feller I was telling you about. He and that kid from New Mexico are the ones who helped us down the canyon with our herd."

Jim and Ned removed their hats and stepped forward, taking Molly's hand, they smiled and said, "Pleased to meet you, ma'am."

"I sent the boys down the canyon to chase them pesky buffalos out of our grazing land. They must be four or five thousand that keep coming back up the canyon. I guess the hunters will find them one of these days, and wipe them out. I kinda hate to see it happen, they're about the only ones left in these parts," Charlie said as they drank their coffee.

"We got a herd left over on the Washita, maybe three thousand head, that we've been trying to save for Quanah and his Comanches. Mostly, the hunters have let them be, but now and again a few are taken by poachers," Jim replied.

"Well, I 'spect you didn't ride all this way to talk about buffalo. What you got on your mind?"

"People and cattle, mostly," Jim answered. "This country is getting downright congested what with all the herds being brought in. I don't know if you realize, but there must be at least five or six ranches which have sprung up, over along the Canadian. And you probably know about that Carhart bunch down on the Salt Fork. Cattle are getting mixed so much, pretty soon no one is going to know who owns what."

Goodnight took a sip of the steaming brew, nodded his head in agreement, before answering. "A couple of days ago, I ran across that Romero sheepherder from Atascosa up on top with a flock of his sheep and he told me about all the cattle being brought in--said they was taking over his grazing country. There hasn't been any of them stray down this far, but I guess it will just be a matter of time before it happens. What are you thinking we should do about it?"

"Well, except for my ranch that the Republic granted to me back in '44, there ain't no property lines. Seems like anyone with a cow is finding a shady spot along the river and establishing a headquarters. Then they turn their cattle loose and let them start grazing in every direction. I know it's free range, and they've got just as much right to the grass as you and me, but I can see it's liable to lead to big trouble if we don't all come to some understanding about who's going to graze where. The last thing we need is a range war."

Goodnight listened attentively, nodded his head in agreement, then said, "We best put out the fire before it gets out of hand."

"That's not the only fire we got brewing, Charlie," Jim said as he sipped his coffee, then turned to Ned, and continued, "Ned, tell Charlie about our run-in with the rustlers."

Ned related the recent adventures he and Billy had with Dutch Henry and the rustlers in Tascosa. When he had finished, Goodnight asked. "I guess you hung 'em to the nearest tree?"

"No, sir. We brought them in to Tascosa and was going to call a jury and try 'em, then hang 'em--but during the night they escaped. We figure they *vamanosed* to New Mexico

Territory, but don't know for certain."

Jim interrupted, "We had wounded that needed attention, so we didn't try to follow them. I don't expect they'll be back any time soon."

"You never can tell," Charlie replied. "They tell me that Dutch is a mean sonofagun. I met him once on the trail. I let him know straight out that I didn't want him messing around in my grazing country and promised to take proper measures with a thirty-thirty if he didn't follow my wishes. He'll probably hide out for a spell then make another try. With all these other herds coming in, he's going to have easy pickins if we don't make plans to stop him."

"That's what Ned and I were thinking. I'd like to get all the ranchers together over at Ceebara and see if we can't make some plans for grazing and patrolling the area."

"Just say when and I'll be there," Goodnight said.

"How about three weeks from today. Me and Ned will ride back to Tascosa and contact all of the ranches along the river if you'll get the Matador bunch and Carhart notified. Might as well bring the women folks along and let them get acquainted."

After giving Hard Tack orders to prepare lunch, Goodnight suggested they ride aways down the canyon and have a look at the new Shorthorn bulls he had brought from Pueblo when he went back after his Molly. Jim and Ned were excited at the prospect, since they planned to bring in some of their own to crossbreed with their longhorns.

The bulls, grazing with a herd of longhorn heifers, were quite a contrast to the long legged, rangey, long horned cows. Mostly reds, whites and roans, they were considerably shorter with thick bodies--and small horns that curved inward towards their ears. Some of them had no horns at all.

"Ain't they the dangdest things you ever seen," Charlie asked, proudly. "The Englishman I bought 'em from says that crossing them with our longhorns will produce a heavier, meatier animal. Said we could expect the horns to be considerably shorter on their calves, and that some of them will be natural muley."

"What you mean, muley?" Ned asked.

"Muley means they won't ever grow any horns, like that big red bull there," as he pointed to a nearby bull which had a rounded forehead and no horns.

"A cow without horns! I'd say that would be a great improvement," Jim replied. "One old cow we bought down in Waco back in sixty-five, nearly broke up our partnership with her six-foot horns. Missed Ned's hind-end by about a quarter of an inch when we put a rope on her."

Charlie laughed, "That's happened to a lot of cowboys, and some of them weren't that lucky. I remember the first drive me and Loving made up the Pecos, one old cow got on the peck, knocked one of my boy's horse down, then rammed her horn clean through his gut. We buried him along the banks of the Pecos."

They rode through the herd, admiring the new bulls, then returned to the dugout.

The Goodnight cowboys rode into camp just before sundown, and were greeted by the smell of a beef hindquarter being barbecued over a mesquite fire. Most of Hard Tack's cooking was done in the shade of a huge cottonwood tree next to the dugout. The cowboys continued to bed down under the stars, as they did while on the trail from Colorado. A bunk house was being constructed, but as yet was unfinished.

They all greeted Ned as if he was a long lost brother, shaking his hand and slapping his back. Ned introduced Jim to the bunch, and they sat around Hard Tack's campfire until after midnight, discussing the changes being made on the *Llano Estacado*.

Daylight found Ned and Jim in the saddle, climbing the dim trail out of the canyon, and heading for Tascosa. Dropping off the plains into the Canadian River Valley, they rode into the small frontier town just at sundown, and pulled up at the Romero Plaza.

Don Casimiro Romero greeted them as they dismounted and invited them into his spacious adobe hacienda.

"You will spend the night with us," he announced, not asking, but ordering.

Jim smiled and answered, "You are too kind, Senor. But we would be honored to once more infringe on your hospitality. Perhaps some day we can repay your kindness if you will visit our ranch."

"And what is the reason for your visit this time, Colonel? I hope it is not rustlers that are responsible."

"No, Senor. It seems that every cattleman in Texas has taken a hankering to start grazing their herds in the Panhandle. Ned and I have just come from visiting with Charlie Goodnight in the Palo Duro. We decided to try to get the new folks all together at Ceebara headquarters and try to divide up the grass peaceably before it develops into a range war," Jim explained.

Romero nodded his agreement. "Perhaps you can convince them that we sheep men also need grass for our sheep. Already we have had cowboys shooting up our herds and even threatening our herders. They say this is cow country and we should take our sheep back to New Mexico. But we have been grazing this land with sheep for many years, even before you and Senor Ned brought the first cattle in."

Jim agreed, and said that the sheep men should be a part of the planned meeting, invited him and his neighbors to attend.

As they sat around the huge fireplace after supper, discussing the situation, Romero instructed his daughter, Piedad, to bring his best wine for his guests. After pouring the wine, Piedad asked politely about Miguel, and Ned could see that her interest was more than that of a friend.

"Miguel is fine," he replied, "and I'm certain he will be spending much time riding the west pasture in order to visit Tascosa frequently."

Piedad blushed as she smiled and returned to the kitchen.

In response to Jim's question about the location of the headquarters of new ranches in the Tascosa vicinity, the Mexican sheep man drew a rough map of the area, pinpointing several spots along the river where cow camps had been established.

"Major Littlefield, with the LIT brand, was in Tascosa today, buying supplies. I believe he is camped down by the spring, next to Henry Kimball's blacksmith shop."

"Good! I'll make him a visit first thing in the morning," Jim said.

* * * * * * * *

Bat Masterson had been elected Sheriff of Ford County, Kansas (Dodge City) in 1878. At the same time, Dutch Henry had been arrested for horse stealing in Trinidad, Colorado. Bat, using his influence, had Dutch extradited to Dodge City to face charges of horse stealing three years earlier. *The Dodge City Globe* printed this tale of the trial.

"This will be a great surprise to many people of the west who received the news of his capture with manifestations of joy and gladness. His fame as a horse thief extends far and wide. He is a star in his particular line. Many a tale of his reckless daring have we listened to with eager interest. How handy he was with his revolver, and with what magnetic influence he governed his confederates. How he rode on a magnificent sorrel horse at the head of his little band, with the solemnity and dignity of a general; and with what alacrity his commands were obeyed. How he had evaded the law. How desperately he had fought when hotly pursued, and how he had always escaped his captors. He was the 'Rob Roy' of the plains and his exploits were only equaled by 'Sixteen-String-Jack' in his palmiest days. He was brought into court last Thursday looking as calm and serene as the noonday sun. The defense closed, the jury retired, and were out but a few moments. The Judge received the paper upon which the verdict was written. The eager audience waited with expectant countenances. Judge Peters unfolded the paper and read, '*Not Guilty*'. Addressing Henry, the Judge said: 'Mr. Henry Borne, the jury have found you not guilty, you are therefore released from custody. 'I thank you , Judge, and you too, gentlemen of the jury.' said Henry, and was off like a shot. Making his way down stairs he hastened to the back door of the courthouse where a fleet steed, saddled and bridled, awaited him. He departed to parts unknown."

The *parts unknown* was south to the Texas Panhandle,

where he and his 'little band' would resume their lucrative profession of horse stealing and cattle rustling. And headquarters for the business would be Tascosa, which was replacing Mobeetie as the toughest town in the west, with numerous saloons, gambling dens, and prostitutes--and no organized law.

With no law to worry about, and with Ceebara cowboys riding herd eighty miles to the east, Dutch believed that his activities would be safe in Tascosa.

Fortunately for him, he and his gang were holed up at his hideout on the Rita Blanca, branding a new batch of rustled cattle, when Ned and Jim came into Tascosa looking for Major Littlefield.

* * * * * * * *

"Major Littlefield, my name's Jim Cole, and this is my partner, Ned Armstrong. We own the Ceebara ranch over on Red Deer Creek," Jim said as he dismounted and stepped up to the camp fire under the huge cottonwood tree on the south side of Tascosa.

Littlefield, smiling, shook Jim's hand and said, "Glad to meet you, Colonel. I've heard a lot about you and Ned and been wanting to make your acquaintance."

They stood around the fire, drinking coffee and discussing cattle prices, grazing conditions, and the changes being brought about in the area with the removal of the buffalo and the Indians.

Changing the subject, Jim said, "Major, Ned and me been checking our ranges for the past week and we found cows carrying your brand, Bugbee's Quarter Circle T, Lee's LE , Torrey's Bar T, and Morgan and Harp's Turkey Track, scattered

190

amongst our cows. Seems to me that's going to develop into a considerable problem when we start roundup in the fall."

"I 'spect you're right, Colonel, but I don't see what can be done about it. This is all open, free range. The grass belongs to the first cow that can eat it, and these mangy longhorns are going to roam wherever the grass is best."

Jim, looking Major Littlefield squarely in the eye, replied, "Sure, a lot of it is free range, but the Republic gave me a grant of nigh onto a million acres back in 1844, and I've got papers showing ownership of a track from the Canadian to the Red and from Mobeetie to Adobe Walls. We've got over twenty-five thousand head grazing that area and hope that you and the other ranchers would recognize our boundaries and do your best to keep our herds separate."

Littlefield reached into his shirt pocket, pulled out a can of tobacco and paper and began rolling a cigarette, while digesting the information he had just learned. He struck a match and lit the cigarette before replying.

"I didn't know that, Colonel. I supposed this whole damned country was open range now that the redskins has been pushed back into Indian Territory," he said. "But even if you do have claim to a million acres, how we going to keep our cattle from straying onto your property? There ain't no fences or markers saying where your property begins."

"I guess the best we can do is call all the ranchers together for a meeting and kinder lay out some grazing ranges and then do our best to keep our herds within those ranges," Jim replied, then added. "Hell, I know we ain't going to be able to keep some of our cattle from mixing, but if we don't do something to try to keep the problem to a minimum, we could end up with a range war that nobody wants."

"You're right, Colonel. I'm willing to cooperate--what do you propose?"

"I spoke to Charlie Goodnight over in the Palo Duro, and we set up a meeting at my ranch house for a week from next Thursday. If you will notify anyone running cows west and north of Tascosa, me and Ned will catch those down the river on our way back to the C Bar A."

"Alright, Colonel. I appreciate you taking a lead in this situation. No need in us waiting until tempers start flaring. I'll be there and bring everyone in these parts with me."

"If you've got any women folks in your camps, bring them along. Belle and Kate would be glad to make their acquaintance," Jim said, then added. "We've got another problem developing which you should be aware of, Major. We had a run in with some rustlers a few weeks ago, so you might need to watch your herds pretty closely. With all these new brands showing up and cattle pretty much running wild, they might start cutting our herds again."

"Thanks, Colonel. We'll keep a sharp eye out."

* * * * * * * *

Hacks, buggies and horsebackers began arriving at the ranch on Wednesday, some having traveled as far as one hundred twenty-five miles. Jim had arranged an area just below the compound, along the spring, as a campground, and it was soon bristling with tents and lean-tos beneath the spreading branches of the huge cottonwood trees.

Pits had been dug, barbecue fires set, and several carcasses of young beeves and buffalo were covered and were slowly cooking in preparation for the huge meeting on Thursday.

Ceebara cowboys had been moved from the bunkhouse, the building cleaned and scrubbed and made ready for the visiting ladies who were arriving from surrounding ranches. Molly Bugbee was the first to ride in with her husband, Tom. Then Colonel Goodnight and his wife, Molly, a name which seemed to be common among the ladies of the plains, arrived in their buggy, which was pulled by a pair of beautiful dappled gray geldings. Henry Campbell of the Matador, and his wife Lizzie, who had joined up with the Goodnight's at Clarendon, arrived in their surrey.

Soon, other ranchers began arriving, most bringing their wives--and a few bringing lady friends which they were courting from Tascosa and Mobeetie. They may have been *painted ladies* in their respective towns, but here they were welcomed and treated with respect.

The group of Mexicans, led by Don Casimiro Romero, arrived in buggies, dressed in their brightly colored clothing and wearing huge sombreros. Miguel was first to welcome them and assisted the beautiful Piedad as she stepped down from the buggy.

"*Bienvenido, Senorita,*" he said, removing his hat.

Piedad smiled and replied, "*Gracias,* Miguel."

Ned had hired a group of musicians from the saloons in Mobeetie, and as the sun set in the west, the sound of fiddles, guitars and banjos echoed back from the walls of the caprock. Soon, the hard packed ground in the middle of the ranch compound was being packed even harder by dancing feet as the men swung their ladies to the beat of the music.

The first dance on the frontier in the Texas Panhandle had begun--and continued until the wee hours of the morning.

The next day the men all gathered in the shade of the huge cottonwood tree which shaded the veranda of the ranch house, and plans were set forth to put some organization into the grazing dilemma.

"Men," Jim said, as the meeting began, "I have asked you all here to discuss, and hopefully, agree on grazing rights of each ranch. This is a big country, probably as many as ten million acres on top of the *Llano Estacado*, and an equal amount below the caprock. There's enough grass for every-one, but without a survey or fences, and no local government, I can anticipate that we will have serious problems that could develop into an all-out range war.

"I've heard that a feller named Glidden has come up with a wire that has barbs on it that does a pretty good job of keeping cattle from straying. Some of the ranchers down around San Antonio have been using it. If we had something like that, we could build a couple of drift fences across the plains which would at least keep the cattle from straying too far."

Tom Bugbee spoke up, "Jim, how many head do you think has been brought in?"

"Littlefield tells me he has about seventeen thousand head grazing the area just east of Tascosa, Torrey has about twenty-five thousand, our C Bar A has over twenty-five thousand, your Quarter Circle T has over five thousand, Goodnight says they're running over ten thousand, and," turning to Bill Lee, he asked, "how many head you running west of Tascosa, Bill?"

"Hard to say, Jim. We drove in fourteen thousand, and had a good calf crop last year--maybe twenty thousand head."

"How about the LX, Deacon, how many head you running?"

"Maybe ten thousand, Jim," Deacon Bates responded.

Henry Campbell of the Matador spoke, "Mark me down for twelve thousand, Jim. Maybe more. I bought eight thousand jingle-bobs from John Chisum over in New Mexico and picked up a few small herds down south on the *Llano.*"

"How about you, Reverend, how many head on the Half Circle Heart?"

"We're just now getting it stocked, Colonel. We plan on running at least seven thousand head."

Turning to Romero, Jim asked, "How many sheep are you folks running , Casimiro?"

"With those of my family, the families of Sandoval, Trujillo, Garcia, Valdez and Sierna--maybe fifty thousand, all together."

Jim tallied the figures, looked around the group, and said, "That's well over a hundred thousand head of cattle and fifty thousand sheep, men--and that's not counting the Bar CC and Turkey Track."

Some of the men whistled their astonishment at the figures. Ned, who had said nothing, spoke. "Here's the problem, men. Most all of your ranches are headquartered along the Canadian and Red, because of the scarcity of water on the plains. That means that many of your boundaries overlap. The LX is on Pitcher Creek and just a short distance west is the LIT at Tascosa which overlaps the LE. Tom's Quarter Circle T is just across the river from the C Bar A, and his east line and Hank's Bar CC west line overlap. The Reverend's and Goodnight's line is nothing but a mark in the grass. Now how long is it going to be before we start jawing about who owns what? Not only that, we've already got our herds scattered and mixed and it's going to be hell just getting them separated at roundup time. Just let some of our hands start accusing someone of running a hot iron and there'll be shootings for sure."

In May, 1876, the Texas legislature had divided the Panhandle area into 55 counties and attached them all to Clay County, with Henrietta as the county seat. Now, thirteen years later, nothing had been done to officially organize those counties--and they were so far removed form Henrietta, that that fledgling frontier town could do nothing to enforce the laws of the state.

Everyone nodded in agreement and Charlie Goodnight spoke. "Looks to me like the first thing we need to do is get the state to send up surveyors, lay off some property lines and get these counties organized."

"That's true, Charlie," Jim responded, "but you know how slow government moves, that's going to take time. We need a plan that we can implement immediately."

Unrolling a large parchment on a table which had been set up in the middle of the group, he continued. "Ned drew us up a rough map of the area, showing the rivers, creeks and canyons. I'd like for each of you to look it over, and to the best of your knowledge, mark off what you consider your grazing range."

The men gathered around the table and, after close scrutiny of the map, began marking their areas. Many of them overlapped, especially those who had established headquarters along the Canadian River, and arguments erupted as to who had first claim.

Romero, realizing that the sheep men were far outnumbered in men and guns, agreed to keep the sheep west and south of Tascosa, along the New Mexico border. He also recognized that their days in Texas were numbered and that they would eventually be forced to push their herds back into New Mexico Territory, or sell them and take up other occupations.

This group of men were all tough, frontiersmen--self made--and were not used to being told what to do and how to do it. Many of them were uneducated or self-educated, but very smart businessmen. They knew cattle, and cows were their business. Most of them had been in the saddle all their lives and had made many trips up the trail with their longhorns to Wichita, Abilene and Dodge City. Some had even trailed herds all the way north to Montana. They had fought Indians, chased buffalo and hung rustlers to build their cattle empires--and were wary of making deals that might require them to give up grass which they considered their own.

When it looked as if the meeting was going to erupt in gunplay, Charlie Goodnight pounded the table with his fist and said, "Now listen, men, fighting ain't going to solve anything. Like Jim said, this is all free range, and don't belong to any of us. Until the state steps in and makes a survey, we're going to have to learn to live and work together. We know we can't keep these 'horns separate--no fences and no markers. Looks to me like this map of Ned's makes sense, long as each one of us recognizes that in a few areas we're going to be running our cows with neighbor's cows.

"I know none of you is going to try to put your brand on my cows, and I hope you know that I'm not going to be putting my brand on yours. Looks like the only solution is to do our best to ride our perimeters and try to keep our herds from mixing, then in the spring and fall, we'll all have cooperative roundups and each of us can cut out our brands and drive them back to our headquarters."

Deacon Bates spoke, "I agree with Charlie. We can all help each other in the roundups, and if we've got cattle that strayed, then it's going to be our individual responsibility to drive them back to our range. We can even help each other in marking and branding the calves, so that whatever brand the mama is carrying will be burned on her calf."

Major Littlefield interrupted Bates. "I think you're right, Deacon, but seems to me we're overlooking a big problem. They's lots of herds being driven across this country, headed for New Mexico, Colorado and Montana. Just last week, a herd came across my country headed for Montana, and before I knew it, they was mixed with my cattle. Luckily, my foreman caught them before they got through, held them up and cut out my brands. Legalized rustling, I calls it."

"Seems to me we best form us an association and hire a few range detectives to take care of that problem," Goodnight said. "If we all chip in, maybe ten cents a cow, it wouldn't cost any of us much. Maybe we could lay off a trail that these South Texas herds could use that wouldn't pass right through our grazing range. That'd keep them from getting mixed with our cattle, and maybe help keep down tick fever from spreading in our herds."

"Good idea, Charlie," Jim said. "Any objection?"

No one voiced objections, and Jim continued. "Alright, it's agreed. What'll we call the organization?"

"Seems to me, Panhandle Stock Association of Texas would be good as any," Bugbee said, "and I say we elect Colonel Goodnight as president."

"Any objections?" Jim asked.

With no objections being voiced, Jim said, "Alright, Gentlemen, we have an association and a president. Let's stand agreed that we all support the association, with our money, our cowboys and our influence. We've already had problems with rustlers and I can see that this problem is going to continue to get worse, with that tough bunch that's taken over Mobeetie and Tascosa."

"As your new president, I'd like to appoint Ned Armstrong to take over as temporary head of the rangers until we can hire a professional," Goodnight said. "How about it Ned, you know the area better than any of us. Are you willing?"

"As long as it's temporary, Colonel. And if each one of the ranchers will lend me one good man to help patrol the area."

"Alright, gentlemen. There's plenty of beef and buffalo simmering in the pits, and with our business over, I say we celebrate. Looks like our ladies is enjoying visiting so much we may not get them to stop yapping for a month of Sundays. We got musicians and I'll break out the cigars and barleycorn if you think your feet will stand up to a little more dancing."

And so for the next three days the celebration at Ceebara continued with the sound of music and laughing echoing back from the walls of the caprock which rose above Red Deer Creek. Finally, the ranchers, very reluctantly, loaded their families and headed back to their home headquarters.

Friendships had been made and renewed--and a shooting war over grazing rights had been averted. But the war with rustlers was just beginning.

13

It was nearing dusk when a lathered sorrel gelding loped into the Ceebara compound carrying a small cowboy. The cowboy was wearing two colts strapped low on his thighs and had a thirty caliber Winchester shoved into the saddle boot. The bullet loops in his belt were full. Dust and sweat streaked his shirt.

He dismounted the sorrel as Belle came to the door of the ranch house.

"Howdy, Miss Belle," he said as he tied his horse to the hitching rail.

"Well, Billy Bonney, what brings you to these parts? I thought you was back in New Mexico."

Stepping onto the porch, Billy removed his hat, smiled and took Belle's hand. "It's a long story, Miss Belle, and I 'spect the Colonel and Ned would like to hear it."

"Come on in, Billy. Jim and Ned are just beginning their supper. I'm sure you must be hungry, looks like you've had a long ride."

"Yes, ma'am, I'd appreciate it."

Jim, Ned and Kate stood as Billy and Belle entered the

dining room, and shook hands with the Kid. Young Cole ran to Billy's side with a smile on his face. Like most eleven year olds, he looked with wonder on the men who had a reputation of being a gun slinger. The Kid spoke to him and tousled his hair. "Now ain't you something, Cole--you're going to be grown before we know it!"

"Glad to see you, Kid," Ned said, and smiling, added, "I wouldn't have thought of you for a hundred dollars. Thought you'd be helping Chisum deliver those cows to the army."

"Now, we can ask Billy questions later. He's had a long ride and looks to me like he's about starved. Billy, step to the back porch and wash up before these vittles get cold," Belle said.

Returning to the table, the Kid took a seat next to Ned and Kate set a plate full of steak and beans in front of him.

"Thank you, Miss Kate," he said as he hungrily began to eat.

"So what brings you back to Ceebara, Kid?" Ned asked after the meal had been completed.

"Trouble, Ned--big trouble," the Kid said. "After I returned to Lincoln when I left Tascosa, Mr. Chisum wanted me to help out his friend, Mr. Tunstall, who was having trouble with Mr. Dolan and Mr. Riley, who own the general store in Lincoln. You remember I was telling you how Dolan and Riley pretty well control all the cattle contracts with the government, and Mr. Chisum and Mr. Tunstall was trying to get some of the contracts. Well, Dolan and Riley are trying to take over the whole territory. They said Mr. Tunstall owed them some money and got a court order to seize some of Mr. Tunstall's horses as payment.. Mr. Tunstall said he didn't owe

201

the money, and refused to let them have the horses, so Mr. Dolan had Sheriff Brady send out a posse to get the horses. Sheriff Brady is the biggest crook in Lincoln County and does everything that Dolan and Riley tell him to do.

"When the posse rode up to the ranch, me and some more of the hands could see that they were up to no good, and we tried to get Mr. Tunstall to leave before he got arrested, but he wouldn't go with us. He rode out to the posse and told them to get off his property. Well, sir, that *hijo de perra*--excuse me Miss Belle--Bill Morton pulled his gun and shot Mr. Tunstall in the head and killed him, right there on his own property-- and Mr. Tunstall wasn't even armed."

"Oh, my stars!" Kate gasped, and laid her hand on Billy's arm.

"Mr. Tunstall had been real good to me, Colonel, treated me like I was his own son--even gave me a horse and saddle. He hired me to kinda guard his cattle 'cause he figured Dolan and Riley was up to no good and was going to try to steal some of them. I felt real bad because me and the boys had not rode out with him when he met the posse."

Billy wiped a tear from his eye and continued. "Him and you was about the only folks that ever treated me like I was somebody, so when Dick Brewer, Mr. Tunstall's foreman, formed a posse to hunt down Bill Morton, I joined him. We finally captured Morton on the Rio Penasco and was taking him and another deputy sheriff back to Lincoln to charge them for the killing of Mr. Tunstall. When they tried to escape, I shot them both--killed 'em deader'n hell. But a couple members of the posse say I shot them in cold blood, that they wasn't trying to escape. They got what they deserved, but now

I've got a price on my head in New Mexico for killing two deputies."

Jim, Ned, Belle and Kate sat stunned as the Kid related his story. Finally, Jim said, "Kid, sounds to me like you had legitimate reasons for doing what you did, and you've got witnesses to back you up. Seems to me you'd best return to Lincoln and give yourself up, otherwise you're going to be running the rest of your life."

"I'd like to, Colonel, but you just don't understand the situation. Dolan and Riley have got the law in Lincoln County and in the Territory in their hands, and ain't no way I could get a fair trial. They intend to put Mr. Chisum and all the other smaller ranchers out of business and take over the whole territory," Billy responded.

"What you think we can do to help, Kid?" Ned asked.

"Ain't nothing you can do, Ned. I didn't come here for help--I just wanted to tell you what happened before you got the story from someone else. They are saying I'm a cold-blooded murderer, and anyone who tries to help me now, is just asking for trouble themselves."

"What are you going to do, Billy?" Kate asked, concerned.

"I'm riding back to Lincoln and help Mr. Chisum. Dolan and Riley are bringing in gunmen to back them up, and Mr. Chisum is going to need all the help he can get. War has already broke out."

"Kid, I think you need to clear your name first," Jim said. "Why don't you ride to Santa Fe and talk to Governor Wallace--I understand he's a fair man. Tell him the story you've told us and I believe he'll help clear your name."

"O.K., Colonel, I'll do that just as soon as we get things

settled in Lincoln County. Right now, I think I owe Mr. Chisum all the help I can give him. I guess I'll be riding out in the morning."

The Kid rode out as promised, but didn't go directly to New Mexico. He didn't tell Jim and Ned everything. After the shooting when he killed the two deputies, he put together a small gang--mostly men who had been riding for Tunstall--and began stealing horses and cattle from the Dolan clan. He and his gang had brought a herd of stolen horses to Tascosa to sell to the cowboys and buffalo hunters. Leaving the other members of his gang in Tascosa, he had ridden to Ceebara to tell his story to Jim and Ned.

Leaving the ranch, he rode back to Tascosa, and after spending a few nights in the wild town, drinking, gambling and consorting with the saloon ladies, the Kid decided they needed to replenish their bankroll. Remembering how easy it had been for Dutch's gang to rustle cattle off the plains, and after seeing all the new brands on the cattle along the Canadian River, he decided to take a herd back to New Mexico and sell them.

The next morning, they rode back east and started gathering a herd of longhorns south of the Canadian River.

"No C Bar A brands, boys," he said, "there's plenty of LIT's and LE's to pick from. We'll head them south a ways, to stay clear of any range riders, then west to Las Vegas. They'll bring us a good price around the mining towns."

With three hundred head of fat , three year old steers gathered, they headed for New Mexico.

* * * * * * *

While the meeting was going on at Ceebara headquarters on Red Deer Creek, Dutch Henry was once again busy building his herd north of Tascosa. Setting up a camp in a secluded canyon off of Rita Blanca Creek, he began gathering cattle along the Canadian and converting them to new ownership.

His running iron was kept hot as they changed L E to Square B, L I T to Square T, and C Bar A to X Triangle A--he had determined that Circle Cross Triangle could no longer be used on cattle which he would sell in the Kansas market.

With a thousand head re-branded, he headed them towards Dodge City. His plans were that when he reached the Arkansas River west of Dodge City, he would divide the herd into three groups, according to brands, and have his hired hands take them in separately. He planned to steer clear of Vince Abercrombie, the cattle buyer who had purchased his first herd of rustled cattle.

With the plains cleared of Indians, and good weather prevailing, they made the drive without incident, arriving in Dodge City at the same time that three large herds came in on the Chisholm Trail. A half-dozen brands were burned into the hides of each of the South Texas herds, and with so many cattle arriving at the same time, no one paid much attention to brands. Dutch was able to dispose of his illegal herd without question.

Paying off his men, he returned to Tascosa.

* * * * * * * *

The area around Las Vegas was booming. Gold had been

discovered above the Cimarron on Mount Baldy, and Elizabethtown sprang up at the foot of Mount Wheeler. Prospectors flooded the area and were hungry for Texas beef. As the crow flies, Elizabethtown was only two hundred miles northwest of Tascosa and, pushing hard, Billy's gang made the drive in two weeks. They filled their pockets with gold from the sale of the three hundred head and turned their horses towards Lincoln County. Billy the Kid's ride down the outlaw trail had begun, and now there was no turning back.

With over a hundred thousand head of cattle scattered across the huge grasslands of the *Llano Estacado,* the thirteen hundred head of recently stolen cattle would not be missed until roundup time, and maybe not even then.

With the advent of the big ranches, cattle rustling became a lucrative and expanding occupation. Many of the cowboys who had come into the area with the herds, decided that thirty dollars a head beat thirty dollars a month, and started their own illegal herds. Running irons were kept hot and a dozen new brands appeared on the scene.

Ned and his newly formed ranger group had their work cut out for them.

* * * * * * * *

"Ned, Charlie Goodnight sent word that he would like for me to join him on a trip to Austin. Says it's time we put some pressure on the state legislature and the governor to put some organization into our area," Jim said as they were pulling the saddles from their horses, after a hard days ride in the Canadian River pasture. "We're never going to have any law until they turn us loose from Henrietta and let us form our own county. We're carrying a petition down that will allow us to formally organize Wheeler County and attach all the other counties in the Panhandle to it. That way we can elect our own governing body, get us a sheriff and judge, and hang some of these danged thieves and murderers."

"I'm for that, Colonel. Me and the cowboys from the other ranches are trying to stop the rustling, but seems like every drifter in the west has gone into the cattle business, using other people's cattle. Some of the rustlers are cowboys working on the other ranches. We've caught a few, but without a court and judge, about all we can do is run them out of the territory," Ned replied.

Jim nodded as Ned continued. "You remember what Deacon said about trail herds from down south coming through this country? Well, a couple of days ago, we was looking for rustlers over on the Salt Fork, and I spotted this big herd headed north. We rode in with our Winchesters loaded, to check the herd to make certain they hadn't picked up any of the Association's cattle and to tell them what trail to take across our territory. I'm telling you, Colonel, I never before in my life saw anything like that."

Jim looked concern, and asked, "What you talking about, Ned?"

"The trail boss, Colonel. Kinda medium build sort of man, not too short and not too tall, riding a big bay horse and settin' in one of them crazy looking, Mexican saddles. But that's not all--this feller had on a long-tailed black coat that was split up the middle that hung down to his boot tops, kinder like those circuit rider preachers wear, and was wearing the damndest looking hat you ever did see-- a hard, black hat like President Lincoln used to wear--tall and flat topped."

Jim laughed, "Was his cowboys all black and was he wearing a big forty-four tied on his hip?"

"Yes, sir, I was gettin' to that. Every one of his hands was black--he called them his *niggers*."

"*Luke Short*," Jim said, matter-of-factly. "I knew him back before the war--played a few hands of faro with him, down in Fort Worth. I've heard it said that he don't hire anyone but black cowboys to handle his cattle--and that each one of them agrees to two things when he hires them--one, that they always call him *Mister* Short; and two, that no one quits his job until the drive is finished. Failing to do either, *Mister* Short promised they would receive a bullet from that big hog-leg strapped to his hip.

"Don't let his looks fool you, Ned. Luke is one tough hombre, not afraid of anything or anyone, and there's many a gun-slinger that questioned his ability that's six-feet under to-day. I hope you didn't push him too hard."

"No sir, I just told him about our troubles with rustlers and passing herds and asked him if he'd mind if we rode through his herd and looked for strays. He said he didn't mind at all, as long as we didn't excite them too much. It wasn't hard to check them--every one had the tip of the left horn bobbed off and a real prominent brand on the left jaw that looked like that plug hat he was wearing."

"What did he say about following the trail we have laid out to keep those south Texas, tick infested cattle out of our herds," Jim asked.

"At first, it looked like he was going to object, but when I

208

explained that we had laid out a shorter route with better watering holes, and had even marked the route by plowing a furrow in the sod all the way across our territory, he said he'd be right proud to oblige. He kinder grinned and said he didn't aim to buck no *Winchester quarantine*, and didn't allow as how his *niggers* would welcome trying to break that quarantine."

Jim laughed, "Sounds like Luke, alright. I'm proud you didn't rile him. He could have been just as ornery as he was agreeable if you'd have riled him."

* * * * * * * *

Jim and Charlie returned from Austin with papers certifying Mobeetie as the county seat of newly formed Wheeler County. Shortly thereafter, a group of citizens, meeting in one of the saloons one night, began to discuss the political situation of their frontier town.

Tom O'Loughlin, on whose land the town site of Mobeetie had been built, and who owned the only cafe in town, chaired the meeting. "Now that we've got us a county, it's time we elected some official leaders,"he said.

Laughing, Mark Husleby, a former mess sergeant at Fort Elliot, and owner of one of the two hotels in Mobeetie, said, "Where at in hell are we going to find people willing to try to govern this wild-eyed town. Maybe get us a *painted up lady* for mayor from one of the cat houses over on Featherbed Hill, a sheriff out of that bunch of gunslingers that spend their time drinking and gambling in the saloons along Main Street--and a judge from the buffalo hunters camped along Sweetwater Creek."

Everyone around the table laughed at the thought.

Uncle Johnny Long, proprietor of the J.J. Long General Merchandise Store, spoke up. "I guess we'll have to do with what is available, but we probably got better choices than that. All of you know Emmanuel Dubbs--buffalo hunter who was with Dixon and Masterson at Adobe Walls when the Indians tried to take it--came here with the first hide hunters, and later filed on a piece of ground out northeast of town. Seems to be a fairminded sort of feller, brought his wife and kids down from Kansas and seems to be committed to staying. He'd probably make a pretty good judge."

Other's around the table nodded in agreement, knowing full well that Emmanuel Dubbs didn't know a blessed thing about what a judge was supposed to do.

When the subject of sheriff came up, everyone was at a loss as to who might be willing to take on such a dangerous position.

Henry Fleming, owner of one of the saloons, and who was noted to keep down violence in his domicile with a double barreled shotgun, was suggested by Henry Frye.

"I doubt he'd take it," Uncle Johnny said. "But we can ask him."

He did, and so a buffalo hunter judge and a saloon operator sheriff were elected to try to bring peace and tranquility to the last frontier in the state of Texas, the rough and tough Texas Panhandle.

13

Sheriff Fleming, although legally in charge of the law in all fifty four unorganized counties in the Panhandle, seldom was seen outside of Wheeler County--there was enough lawlessness in Mobeetie to keep him and his one deputy busy.

Judge Dubbs, having no knowledge of the law, immediately dragged the newly formed *government* into hot water by having Sheriff Fleming arrest a Deputy U.S. Marshall from Dallas who had suddenly appeared in Mobeetie and started arresting local citizens on trivial charges of breaking the law. After thirty-five locals had been arrested and jailed by the Marshall, Dubbs ruled the arrests to be illegal and released the prisoners.

However, the marshal prevailed on the commanding officer at Fort Elliot to assist in re-arresting his prisoners, loaded them in wagons and, with an army escort, headed for Dallas. Dubbs, not to be pushed around by "outside influences", formed a posse and took after the wagons. In the dead of night, with loaded buffalo guns, the posse surprised the marshal's caravan, once again released the prisoners and arrested the marshal and his men.

The next day in court, Judge Dubbs charged the marshal and his men with contempt of court and fined each one of them $100 "plus trimmins," which amounted to $120 in all.

Judge Dubbs, fearing a vigilante committee was being organized for a lynching party with the marshal as invited guest, sent the federal lawmen packing out of Mobeetie, and warned them not to come back.

However, a few weeks later, the marshal returned from Dallas with a U.S. government official and arrested the judge and sheriff for "interfering with officers of the United States Government in discharge of duties."

Jim and Ned, in town for supplies, joined Uncle Johnny Long, Mark Huselby and other local citizens, in an effort to secure the release of Dubbs and Fleming. However, the judge convinced them that he would get justice in Dallas, and agreed to accompany the marshal as his "prisoner."

All of the original prisoners were re-arrested by the marshal, and the large group, in wagons and under military guard, once again headed for Dallas, four hundred miles to the south.

The United States Marshal and his *U.S. Government Official*, however, did not reckon with the attitude of down-state citizens. The story of Judge Dubbs and Sheriff Flemings' plight had preceded them, and Judge Plemmons with a group of citizens greeted them in Henrietta, vowing to stick by them in what they considered illegal interference by the U.S. Government in local law.

Plemmons and his delegation accompanied the group to Dallas where the mayor and a welcoming committee, having heard of the affair, met them, and announced their support of the buffalo hunter judge and the saloon operator sheriff.

The mayor, General William Cabell, as spokesman of the welcoming committee, announced, *"We have come to greet you and to show you that Dallas is bitter at the treatment accorded you. We honor the men of the Panhandle who are brave enough to do their duty even when their actions will antagonize men who have power, and who use that power unjustly."*

After being treated royally by the citizens of Dallas over the weekend, the group was brought to trial. The court ordered all prisoners released and each were paid $2.50 per day for the time they had been under arrest.

The marshal and his men were then arrested, tried and given jail sentences for their part in the illegal arrests.

Judge Dubbs, Sheriff Fleming and the thirty-five citizens of Mobeetie returned home and were welcomed as heroes.

* * * * * * * *

Even with the Panhandle Stock Association's rangers patrolling the area, huge numbers of cattle were disappearing without a trace. The area was so large and the cattle so numerous, it was virtually impossible to stop the stealing. Ned suspected, accurately, that many of the cattle were being stolen and burned with a running iron by men who worked on the ranches.

"Colonel," he said one day as they were discussing the problem, "I know danged well that the foreman of the LX is in cahoots with the rustlers, but I can't prove it. I told Deacon about my suspicions and he got plumb out of sorts--said I didn't know what I was talking about."

Jim pondered the problem before answering, removed a plug of tobacco from his shirt pocket and bit off a chew. "Do you think he's taking any of our cows?' he asked.

"No, sir. Looks to me like he's keeping his men away from certain areas of their own grazing grounds and letting the rustlers cut out what they want. I can't figure if he's being paid for his cooperation or if the cattle are being put on grass over in New Mexico and he's building himself his own herd."

"Well, if Deacon trusts him, and he's just stealing LX cows, then I guess there's not much you can do about it until you catch him in the act."

What Ned did not know, was that Dutch Henry's gang was back in business, and he was paying the LX foreman to keep his men away from the area where he was gathering his next herd to be sold in Dodge City.

Having completed his herd, Dutch hit the trail to the Rabbit Ears grazing area to rest up the cattle and let the doctored brands heal up. At the same time, another meeting of the ranchers was called by Major Littlefield to be held in Tascosa. Most of the cattlemen attended. When they had all arrived, Littlefield opened the meeting.

"Men," he said, "I'm fixin' to start my roundup so I can get my steers into Dodge before the snows start to flying. I know there's a lot of you feller's cattle mixed in with mine, so I felt I'd better let you know. We'll be rounding up north and south of the river and driving to my pens at headquarters starting next Monday. Seems to me if we would all pitch together, we could make my roundup, then move on down the river, and roundup Deacon's, Tom's and Jim's herds and separate them according to brands. Once we get the Canadian River herds separated, we could all head south and help Charlie and Hank get their herds together."

"Sounds like good thinking to me," Goodnight said. "I've noticed a lot of your brands mixed in with our cattle, and I'm sure some of mine are in with yours. We've been grazing that area west of the canyon along the *Tierra Blanca* and there's been a lot of strays coming down from the north and mixing with my herd."

After a long discussion, a schedule was agreed upon. Crews from different ranches would meet and have a cooperative roundup, the different brands separated and the cattle driven back to their home ranches. The LIT, LX, and LE herds would be gathered to a central location at Tascosa; Quarter Circle T, Bar CC, Turkey Track, and C Bar A cattle would be gathered at the old Adobe Walls ruins; JA and Matador cattle would be gathered at a spot where the two ranches joined, just below the caprock.

With over five hundred men sweeping the prairies and canyons in the cooperative roundup, the cattle were gathered, separated, marked and branded in less than a month and moved back to their home pastures.

A rough tally by Ned indicated that the Ceebara herd was once again, over a thousand head short. "I'm sure we didn't find all of the cattle that have strayed, Colonel, but looks to me like rustlers have took another cut out of our herd," Ned said, as they watched their cowboys begin cutting out the fat three and four year olds for the drive to Dodge City.

"No doubt about it, Ned," Jim replied. "Maybe now that

we are getting better organized, and now that the governor has agreed to send up some Texas Rangers to help, we'll be able to put a stop to it.."

* * * * * * *

Big Red waded across the belly deep Arkansas and headed for the stockyards, knowing that once more he had brought his herd to the end of the trail. The five thousand head of steers followed him into the pens and Ned closed the gate.

"Well, Colonel," he said, as he removed his hat and wiped the dust and sweat from his forehead, "I'm shore glad to see that last tail inside those pens."

Jim stepped off the big black stallion, smiled and nodded, "Seems like the trail gets longer every year, don't it, Ned. Or maybe it's just that we're getting older."

"I think it's a little bit of both, Colonel," Ned replied, smiling as he looked back down the street, searching for Cole amongst the other trail hands.

Cole had ridden drag all day, and he and his horse were covered with dust as he rode up and dismounted. As soon as he dismounted, the horse shook his body, rattling the saddle and throwing dust and sweat onto Ned and Jim.

"Pa," Cole said, as he removed his hat and began beating his clothes with it, "I'm ready for me a bath and a steak. That dust was something fierce, today."

"Well, how about that Colonel. Here I was trying to think that was just a big old dirt clod on that horses back, and it was Cole all the time," Ned joked as he tousled the boy's hair.

Sonny rode up with a pencil and pad in his hand. "I tallied four thousand, nine hundred and sixty, Colonel. Didn't lose but forty head on the trail. Beats what we did last year."

"Good, Sonny. Tell the hands to check in at the Dodge House, two to a room. After they get cleaned up, the first round of drinks at the Long Branch is on me," Jim said.

"Yahoo!" a couple of the cowboys yelled as they strode down Front Street towards the hotel, their chaps flapping and spurs jingling.

A familiar figure walked across the street and approached Ned and Jim. "Howdy, Vince," Jim greeted, "brought you another batch of good Texas beef--that is, if you're willing to pay a fair price."

Vince Abercrombie, smiling shook Ned's hand then Jim's, and looked at Cole, standing next to the fence. Reaching out, he shook Cole's hand and said, "Well, Jim, I think I'll deal with this cowboy, this year. Looks to me like he's the one doing all the work."

Cole beamed at the compliment and said, "Howdy, Mr. Abercrombie."

Vince climbed the fence, looked the herd over and whistled, "Fatter'n fat hogs, Jim. You must have been feeding this bunch corn all year."

"No, sir," Cole spoke up, "We ain't got any corn, Mr. Abercrombie, but the grass was really good all summer, and it really put on the taller."

"See what I mean, Jim. The boy knows cattle better than you and Ned, both. You boys get cleaned up and I'll treat you to the biggest steak the Dodge House can cook up."

"That's the best deal, we've been offered all day, Vince," Ned said as they turned and started walking towards the hotel.

They moved out of the street and watched as a long train of wagons, pulled by mules, lumbered down the street towards the rail yard, loaded with buffalo hides. "Look there, Pa," Cole shouted. "It's Mr. Dixon driving that wagon."

Sure enough, it was Billy Dixon, and Ned shouted a greeting. "Hey, you consarned mule skinner, where'd you come by all them hides?"

Billy pulled his wagon over and stopped. "Ned Armstrong! You're plumb out of your territory, ain't you?"

Climbing down from the wagon, he stuck his big hand out and shook Ned's. Turning to Jim, he said, "Colonel, damned if it ain't good to see you. How's Miss Belle and Miss Kate?"

"They're fine, Billy, long as they can keep me and the boys out of their hair. How about you? You must be doing alright to bring twenty wagonloads of hides into town."

Laughing, Billy replied, "Wish they was mine, Colonel, but they belong to Charlie Rath. I been down around the Yellow House and Double Mountains hunting all summer. Did right well and brought my hides into Rath's trading post that he set up down on the Brazos. After I sold him all I had, he struck a deal with me to help him haul his hides up here. I was coming anyways, so I figured I might as well get paid for the trip."

It was easy to tell that Billy had been on the frontier for many weeks. His black hair was long, hanging below his shoulders, his beard was long , thick, and untrimmed--and his buckskins were caked with dirt , grime and dried blood. An odor of mule sweat and buffalo hides filled the air around him.

"Well, Billy, we got a lot of talking to catch up on," Ned

said. "Mr. Abercrombie has offered to buy our supper soon as we get cleaned up. Why don't you join us at the Dodge House."

"I'll do that, Ned. Soon's I get these hides down to Rath's wagon yard and give my boys orders to tend to our mules. I 'spect I could use a little soap and water before I try to do any socializing."

Ned smiled and nodded his agreement.

* * * * * * * *

They all took rooms at the Dodge House, bathed then joined Vince in the dining room of the hotel.

"Lose any more cattle to rustlers, this year, Ned?" Abercrombie asked, as they sat down at the table in the Dodge House Restaurant.

"Yes, sir," Ned replied. "Don't rightly know how many, but looks like we come up a thousand or more short at round-up. I 'spect some of them are already on somebody's plate in Chicago by now."

"We've been getting a lot of new brands in, this summer," Vince answered. "Of course, there's been a lot of new ranches established down your way since spring, but some of the herds brought in had some mighty suspicious looking brands. A couple of small herds came in from the west--out of New Mexico, I guess--and those hides could have smelt a hot iron recently. There's still one small herd that's grazing a couple of miles west of town, waiting for an empty pen, but I haven't looked them over, yet.

"I didn't see any more Circle Cross Triangle cattle, but that don't mean they didn't burn a different brand on yours. I guess we've probably shipped three hundred thousand head out already, and you can imagine how many brands were on them--no way we can check to see which ones have been changed with a running iron."

"Have you seen Bat yet, Ned? You know he's been appointed deputy U.S. Marshall for the area. He's in town somewhere, probably over at the Lady Gay playing Monte with Doc Holliday," Dixon said.

"Haven't seen him, Billy, but look forward to it. I knew he had been elected as Sheriff of Ford County, but didn't know he'd taken the marshal's job."

"After we finish these steaks, we'll walk around and see if we can stir him up," Billy said.

Sure enough, Bat Masterson was seated at a table in the corner of the Lady Gay, playing Monte with Doc Holliday and three Texas cowboys.

"Deal me out, boys," he said when he recognized Billy, Ned and Jim approaching. Standing, he walked to meet them with a big smile on his face. "Now if this ain't the ugliest three Indian fighters I ever did see," grabbing their hands and shaking them and slapping them on their backs.

"At least we look like Indian fighters," Ned said as he stood back and looked Bat over. "You look like something the dogs drug back from one of them socialite parties in New York City."

Bat, clean shaven except for a well trimmed mustache, a round topped , small brimmed bowler hat resting at a cocky angle on his head, hair cut short, and dressed in a three piece, expensive woolen suit, did look like an eastern lawyer. However, Ned noticed that he was wearing a gun belt and holster, filled with a beautiful, pearl handled, Colt .45.

Leading them to his table, he introduced them to Doc Holliday and asked the three cowboys to find another table, then yelled at the barkeeper to bring a bottle and three more glasses.

"This is like old-home-week, Bat," Jim said, after the drinks were poured. Holding his glass towards the center of the table, he added, "A toast, to old friends."

The five glasses clinked as they touched in the middle of the table, and the five frontiersmen drank to their friendship.

Even Ned, who seldom touched strong liquor, became inebriated as they sat around the table and talked of their experiences together in the Indian wars, cattle drives and buffalo hunts. They were the last to leave the Lady Gay in the wee hours of the morning, and weaved their way back to the Dodge House.

* * * * * * *

Several cattle buyers were looking over the Ceebara herd the next morning when Jim and Ned finally finished breakfast and returned to the stock pens. Cole, having slipped out of bed at daybreak, had eaten breakfast with Vince Abercrombie and was showing him around the herd.

"Nice set of cattle, Cole," Vince said, treating the eleven-year old as if he was grown. "I 'spect they're going to bring top dollar again this year."

"Yes, sir, Mr. Abercrombie," Cole replied, "and you should see the calves that are on the ground this year from the Durham bulls we put with some of our best cows. In a couple of years, Grandpa says they are going to be the best cattle this country has ever seen."

"Better step out of the way, Cole," Vince said as he saw a new herd coming down the alleyway to be placed in pens at the other end of the stockyard.

They climbed the fence and watched as the cattle moved by. "Ever seen that brand before, Cole?" Vince asked.

"No, sir. I helped with the roundup last month and there was a lot of new brands but I didn't see that one. Looks like an X , a triangle, and an A. Hard to tell though, the hair has growed over it pretty thick."

The last of the herd passed by and was followed by three cowboys who were driving them up the alleyway. One of the cowboys looked familiar to Vince, but he couldn't place him. A barrel of a man, he was clean shaven except for a long, handle-bar mustache which curled at the ends. He was wearing regular trail clothes, tight legging chaps and a huge brimmed, high crowned black felt hat. The hat was pulled low in the front, covering most of his face. His gunbelt was slung low on his hip--more like a gunslinger than like a Texas cowboy. As they rode by, the cowboy looked the other way, hiding his face from Vince and Cole.

"I swear that cowboy looks familiar, Cole, but I can't place where I've seen him. Probably came up with one of the herds I bought from South Texas last year."

They climbed down from the fence, and walked back to the hotel. Ned and Jim were just sitting down for breakfast, looking bleary-eyed and the worst for wear. Cole smiled when he saw the shape his dad and grandad were in.

"Ma told you to watch out for me on this drive, but looks like I'm going to have to watch out for y'all."

Jim laughed at his grandson. "You just remember to keep this to yourself, young man. Don't you go telling your ma and grandma tales about how we act when we get away from home or we won't bring you anymore. Besides, it's all the fault of Billy and Bat, keeping us up all night and forcing that rot-gut down us while they bragged about all them buffalo and Indians they shot down on the *Llano*."

"I've been showing Mr. Abercrombie our herd, Pa. There's probably a half-dozen other buyers looking them over, but Mr. Abercrombie says they're just a bunch of crooks looking to steal our cattle, and we hadn't ought to be talking to them. But looks to me like we should give them all a chance to make a bid."

Vince's face turned red and he said, "Now I was just joshing the boy, Jim. But you know if you want top dollar, you're going to have to sell to the best, most honest cattle buyer in Dodge City--*me*."

Jim laughed, "You old scalawag. You might be able to pull the wool over my eyes, but that grandson of mine is too smart for you."

"Grandpa, while we were down at the pens, another herd came in. Looked like they was carrying as much taller as ours. Wasn't very many of them, maybe four or five hundred head, and they had a funny looking brand. Wasn't from our part of the country because I never did see a brand like that when we were making our roundup last month."

"That's right, Jim," Vince said. "I thought I recognized one of the cowboys but I just couldn't place where I'd seen him before."

"What'd the brand look like, Cole?" Ned asked.

"It was pretty haired over, Pa, but looked to me like an X, Triangle, A."

Pushing a napkin and pen over to him, Ned said, "Draw it for me, son."

Ned and Jim looked the drawing over, and Jim said, "You know, it would be pretty easy to make a C into an X with a running iron. And a straight bar, with just two lines added could be made into a triangle. Maybe we should look at that herd, it might be some of those steers we're missing."

Finishing his steak and eggs, he pushed his chair back and said, "Come along, Cole, you and I will go take a look while Ned sees how many dollars he can squeeze out of this old skinflint for our herd."

They walked to the stockyards and up the alleyway where Cole said he'd seen the new cattle pass. "They took them on up this alley, Grandpa, towards the other end of the stockyard. Shouldn't be over one or two pens of them.

At the east end of the yard, the alleyway turned to the left, and a half-dozen pens were strung out along its outer edge. Five of the pens were empty, and the last one had about four hundred head of fat steers milling inside.

Jim climbed the fence and looked closely at the brand on the nearest steer, a big roan with crooked horns. Like Cole had explained, the brand was haired over and hard to make out. He could see the *triangle* plainly, the *A* looked as if it was an older brand, but he couldn't tell what the front brand was. Another big paint steer pushed his way between Jim and the roan steer, and he could see the front brand plainly. It was an *X* alright, but the arms and legs of the *X* were curved rather than straight. It was really a backward *C* tied to a forward *C*. These were *C Bar A* cattle for certain.

There were three horses tied to the fence, but no cowboys in sight.

"Them's our cattle, Cole," Jim said. "You did good, spotting them that way."

"What we going to do, Grandpa. You want me to open the gate and drive them back down the alley and put them in with our herd?"

"No, Cole. They aren't going anywhere. We'll get the marshal and let him have a look at them. Then we'll try to catch the whole gang when they try to sell them."

* * * * * * * *

"Yep, no doubt about it, Colonel. Those are Ceebara cattle, for sure," Bat said after he had looked them over. "Like you said, they ain't going anywhere, and if we play our cards right, maybe we can round up the entire gang."

"I think what we should do, is push some of our herd down here and fill up these three empty pens, then while my boys are watching our cattle, they can keep an eye out on this herd. When they start to load them on the boxcars, we'll catch them redhanded."

"Alright, Jim. Sounds like a good plan. You let me know when you think we should move in," Bat said.

Walking back to Abercrombie's office, they entered and told Vince about their plans. "Vince, why don't you see if you can deal for that herd, and make certain that they agree to load out the cattle for you. After the loading, and while you are making final payment, we can move in."

"Alright, Jim, I'll see what I can do," Vince said.

* * * * * * * *

Vince made a deal for the cattle, paying half down with the agreement that the other half would be paid after the cattle were loaded. He didn't see the cowboy who he had thought he recognized, but supposed he would be there to help load out the cattle.

On the day the cattle were to be loaded, Bat and Billy, dressed as cowboys, joined Ned, Sonny, and Jim at the pens. They watched as cattle cars were pulled in on the rail siding, and the rustlers began shoving the herd into the cars.

With the loading completed, the cowboys headed for Abercrombie's office and were joined by the one who Vince had thought he recognized. While counting out the money, Vince continued to try to put a name to the face.

Then it dawned on him--*Dutch Henry*, who had sold him the rustled herd of Ceebara cattle the year before. Dutch had shaved his heavy beard and had trimmed his mustache, completely changing his looks. He gave the name of Bart Mathews, when Vince asked what name to put on the Bill of Sale.

Stepping out the door of Abercrombie's office, Dutch and his six cowboys walked towards their horses which were tied to the rail, and Dutch shoved the money into his saddle bags.

"Alright, men," Bat ordered, 'turn around slow with your

hands in the air. You're under arrest for cattle rustling." He, Billy and Ned, stepped out into the street from behind horses tied to the rail about twenty paces from the rustlers.

Dutch turned, dropped to one knee while at the same time, drawing his pistol, and fired. His shot went high, hitting Bat's round bowler hat and knocking it from his head.

The other rustlers dove behind their horses, pulled their guns and began firing. Ned and Billy quickly pulled their revolvers and returned fire.

Before Dutch could regain his balance and fire again, Ned's bullet caught him in the shoulder and knocked him to the ground.

The horses bolted, breaking their bridle reins from the hitching rail, and ran down the street. The outlaws who had taken refuge behind them were left exposed and one of them fell with a bullet from Billy's Colt hitting him in the thigh.

Jim and Cole had been standing on the boardwalk when the action began, expecting a peaceful arrest to be made. When the shooting started, Jim pulled his pistol and in one easy motion, fired and hit the rustler who was immediately behind the prostrate Dutch. He screamed, dropped his gun and grabbed his wrist.

With so much excitement taking place, with dust and smoke in the air, no one saw Dutch roll over, pull his gun up and fire. His shot hit Jim in the chest and knocked him backwards.

As he fell, Jim dropped his gun and reached to cover the spot where the bullet had entered.

Cole, realizing that his grandad had been shot, dropped to his knees beside him, crying, "Grandpa! Grandpa!" Then, without realizing what he was doing, picked up the Colonel's revolver and turned towards the battle.

Dutch had staggered to his feet and was running down the boardwalk towards Jim and Cole, while pointing the barrel of the pistol at Jim, "You one armed old coot, it's payback time for what you did to me in Tascosa last year," he shouted.

Cole, tears rolling down his cheeks, pulled Jim's Colt up, holding it with both hands, and fired, hitting Dutch in the middle of the chest. The recoil of the revolver pushed the boy backwards against the hitching rail.

Through his tears, Cole watched as the huge gunman was knocked backwards, and as if in slow motion, his feet flew up and he fell sprawling on his back, only a few feet from where Jim lay.

Turning back to Jim, Cole dropped the gun and grabbed his grandad's hand and began shaking it. "Grandpa, don't die, please don't die!" he said, then screamed, "Pa, come quick! Grandpa's been shot!"

Ned rushed from the street to where Jim lay, blood covering his chest. He knelt down, placed his hand under Jim's head and raised him to a sitting position, removed his bandana and placed it over the hole. The flow of blood stopped but Ned could see that it was too late, Jim was slowly slipping away.

Jim feebly placed his hand on Cole's shoulder, looked him in the eye, and said, "You did good, Cole, I'm proud of you." His eyes moved to Ned and he said, "The boy used my gun and saved us both, Ned."

Through tear-filled eyes, Cole looked at his grandad and said, "Please don't die, Grandpa--I don't want you to die!"

Raising his eyes to Ned, Jim said, "Tell Belle I'm sorry, and I love her. You take care of the family, son. I don't think I'm going to make it."

He coughed and blood flowed from the corner of his mouth. "If you can figure a way, I would appreciate it if you would take me back to the ranch for burial," he said.

Ned, wiped the tears from his eyes, and replied, "You know I will if it's necessary, but you just hang in there, Colonel, you're going to make it fine."

Jim's hand slowly fell from Cole's shoulder, his eyes closed and he breathed his last breath. Cole sobbed as he picked up Jim's hand and held it to his cheek.

Ned placed his arm around his son's back and pulled him tightly to his chest. "He's gone, son," was all he could say through his sobs.

Bat and Billy herded the other four rustlers out of the street and towards the jail, leaving the two dead ones where they lay. Sonny rushed to Ned's side.

After Ned regained his composure, he stood and looked at the dead renegade who had shot the Colonel, and at first failed to recognize Dutch Henry, who's face was clean shaven except for the handlebar mustache. Then it dawned on him, Dutch had shaved the heavy beard, and changed his looks completely.

"Bat, this is the hombre that we captured down at Tascosa last year for rustling our cattle--Dutch Henry," he said.

"It damned sure is, Ned. I'd of never recognized him if you hadn't told me. I never seen him without that beard before," then added, "Ned, I'm surely sorry about the Colonel."

Sonny knelt by Jim's side, held his hand, as tears flowed down his weathered cheeks. "I loved him as much as I could have if he had been my own father, Ned. Ever since he married Ma, he's treated me as if I were his own son.

"I know what you mean, Sonny. Ever since we met on the battlefield in Virginia, he's been a father to me--the best man I ever knew," Ned replied.

"Ned, I'm taking these hombres to the hoosegow," Bat said. "I'll send the undertaker back with an ambulance to pick Jim up."

* * * * * * * *

General Sheridan, making a tour of forts on the frontier, was at Fort Dodge when the shooting took place. Upon hearing the news, he rode into town to pay his respects to Ned.

"Armstrong," he said as they both stood viewing the body in the undertakers parlor, "the Colonel was a fine gentleman and a great help to me and members of my staff during the Indian wars. If you plan on carrying him back to Texas, I would like to offer the use of an army ambulance and a military escort."

"Thank you, General, I would certainly appreciate that. I figure it will take four days to make the trip, and with the weather as cool as it is, Mr. Collar, the undertaker, tells me formaldehyde will preserve the body for that long. We will be ready to leave in the morning."

"Is there anything else I can do for you. You know that the federal government is at your disposal since you are a recipient of the Congressional Medal of Honor."

"Yes, sir, there's one thing. They tell me that Fort Dodge is connected to Fort Sill and Fort Elliot by telegraph now. I'd like to get a message to the ranch about the Colonel's death, and request Major Biddle to send word to the other ranchers in the area about our plans. Would you see that General Mac-Kenzie and Quanah Parker at Fort Sill are notified, and tell them that we should be arriving at Ceebara with the body in four days. I know that if it is at all possible, Quanah will want to attend."

"Count it as done, Armstrong," the general replied. "I will instruct Major Biddle to personally carry the message to your ranch, and have him send troops to each of the ranches."

"Thank you, General," Ned said as they turned and walked out of the funeral parlor onto Front Street, where a crowd had gathered.

Many in the crowd walked forward to shake Ned's hand and offer their condolences--people who had become close friends to him and Jim during their annual cattle drives. Vince Abercrombie was at the head of the group.

"Ned," Vince said, "I plan on accompanying you back to the ranch. You know what a great friend that Jim was to me, almost like a brother. When do you plan on leaving?"

"Thanks Vince, I appreciate that. We'll be leaving early in the morning. General Sheridan has offered an ambulance and a military escort and I figure we'll be on the trail about four days."

As the general promised, there was an ambulance hitched to four beautiful mules waiting in front of Collar's parlor the next morning. A military escort of four cavalry riders for the front and four at the rear, sat their horses at attention, as Ned, Sonny, Bat and Billy carried the casket from the building.

The two military riders in the front carried flags unfurled, one with the stars and stripes--the other with the Confederate stars and bars--as the funeral cortege moved slowly down Front Street.

Crossing the Arkansas River and heading south down the Ceebara Trail, the procession began to move faster, with the mules and horses held at an easy trot.

Ned, Sonny, Cole, Bat Masterson and Billy Dixon rode immediately behind the rear military escort. Vince Abercrombie, driving his buggy pulled by a span of mules was behind them, and the Ceebara cowboys, with their wagon and chuck wagon brought up the rear.

Thus would they travel for four days across the endless prairie--across the grasslands which Jim had loved so dearly. As they crossed the Canadian River and headed up the Red Deer Creek, it was appropriate that a large herd of gentle buffalo, mixed with a herd of Ceebara longhorns, parted and stood watching as the procession moved by.

As they approached the ranch compound, Ned could see that word of the tragedy had preceded them. Indian tipis were erected below the ranch house in the shade of the huge cottonwood trees. Next to them, several army style tents had been erected, and it was apparent that they were being occupied by ranchers and their families from the surrounding area.

Off to the west of the ranch house, a military camp had been made and one of the tents was flying the flag of General MacKenzie.

As the funeral procession rode up the trail, Ned could see scores of people, Anglo, Mexican and Indians lining the way on both sides of the trail. Entering the compound, the military escort pulled up to the ranch house, where Quanah Parker, dressed in his finest regalia, long war bonnet of Eagle feathers trailing down his back, stood tall and straight, his war lance held firmly in his right hand.

Next to Quanah stood his son, Jim Bold Eagle, also dressed as a warrior of the Comanche nation. Flanked on either side of Quanah and Bold Eagle were General MacKenzie, Major Biddle, and Captain Baldwin.

To their rear stood many of the ranchers of the area--Charles Goodnight, Reverend Carhart, Deacon Bates, Hank Campbell, George Littlefield, Tom Bugbee, Cape Willingham, Casimiro Romero, Bill Lee and several others.

Belle and Kate, dressed in black, stood on the veranda of the ranch house, surrounded by the women of the area, Molly Goodnight, Molly Bugbee, Lizzie Campbell, Piedad Romero and others.

Several residents of Mobeetie stood off to the left, including Judge Emmanuel Dubbs, Sheriff Henry Fleming, Mark Husleby, Uncle Johnny Long, and Tom O'Loughlin. There was also a newcomer with the group who had arrived only days before to assume the responsibilities of District Attorney, Temple Houston. Son of Sam Houston, Temple and Jim had been friends for many years when Jim was a resident in the Houston household.

In the center of the ranch yard stood Jim's faithful ranch crew, the Garcia's, Slim Compton's family, Waddy, Boots, Manuel, and scores of cowboys with their hats held in their hands.

Ned and Cole dismounted and walked to the veranda, where Ned held Belle close and told her how sorry he was that he was unable to prevent this tragedy. Cole had gone to his mother's side, and they both stood crying unashamedly at their loss.

The military escort dismounted, marched stiffly to the rear of the ambulance, opened the door and pulled the coffin out. Six of them, three to each side, carried the coffin up the steps and into the huge living room of the ranch house, setting it in the middle of the room where a sturdy table had been arranged. The flag of the confederacy was draped over the unopened end of the coffin, the stars and stripes on a staff at its head. The military pallbearers stood back three steps on either side and the gathered mourners began to walk into the ranch house, by the coffin to view the body, and out the back door.

A freshly dug grave was open under the huge cottonwood tree, only a short distance from that of the lovely Morning Star, wife of Quanah Parker.

After a short period of mourning for the family, the body was carried to the grave site, the huge crowd of family and friends gathered around and short eulogies were given by General MacKenzie, Quanah Parker, Bat Masterson and Billy Dixon.

The quiet of the moment was shattered as the regiment bugler from Fort Elliot began to sound taps as Jim's cowboys lowered the casket into the grave and began to cover it with the sandy soil of the Red Deer Valley.

No one noticed the lone cowboy, standing on the cliff

overlooking the ranch house, holding his horse and watching the coffin being lowered into the grave. The Kid wiped tears from his eyes as he removed his hat. Turning, he mounted the bay and rode sadly back to the west.

A huge old eagle soared lazily overhead, looking down on the activities which were taking place below his lofty position--the same eagle which had observed the Colonel and Ned, as they arrived at this spot, fifteen years before.

Quanah, who was called the Eagle by his people, looked up when he heard the eagle cry, and watched as it soared away towards the caprock.

"Yes, my friend," he thought to the eagle, *"much has happened in fifteen years since we saw our friend come to our land. The buffalo have been slaughtered, their bones lie dry and white in the grass, the red man has been banished from his hunting grounds, the white man's longhorn cattle are too many to number, and towns are being started where we once pitched our tipis. Our land is no more, it is now the white man's land. Let us hope that he takes better care of the land than he did the buffalo."*

Epilogue

In the years following Colonel Cole's death, many changes took place on the *Llano Estacado*. In the early 1880's, barbed wire was introduced onto the plains, and two drift fences were built by the cattlemen to keep cattle from drifting too far from their home ranges. The fences worked well until 1886, when a strong blizzard drifted the cattle south. Hitting the fences, they could go no further to find shelter. Literally thousands of cattle were found frozen, piled against the fences after the snow melted.

As the lands along the rivers and creeks became settled, cattlemen began to search for methods to secure permanent water on the flat, waterless prairies. Windmills and well drilling rigs proved to be the answer, and soon wind mills sprang up all over the Panhandle, with stock tanks overflowing with pure water pumped from deep under the prairie sod.

The water was a blessing in one sense for the ranchers, but a curse to the cattleman in another--with water came the sod busters, and with the sod busters came state control over grazing rights. A fee for grazing state lands was levied on the cattlemen and much of the lands they had been grazing were filed upon and fenced by the sod busters.

Foreign investors, mostly Scottish and English, pumped money into the area and the privately owned ranches were soon bought out by foreign syndicates. The LIT, Turkey Track, Quarter Circle T, IX, T-Anchor, Matador, and Quarter Circle

Heart became properties of the foreign investors.

Then the state legislature gave three million acres along the Texas-New Mexico line to the Capitol Freehold Land and Investment Company, Ltd. in exchange for the building of the State Capitol Building in Austin. The XIT, covering much of ten counties and reaching for two hundred miles north and south, was born.

Hundreds of thousands of acres of the lush grass lands were given to railroads in exchange for the building of rail lines into the area.

And the cattle ranchers were squeezed from all sides until eventually, most disappeared from the scene.

Billy the Kid continued to steal cattle from the ranches on the Llano Estacado until Pat Garret finally caught him and killed him in Fort Sumner. After the death of the Kid, Garrett was hired by the Panhandle Stockmen's Association as Captain of the Association's rangers, to track down and bring to justice the hundreds of cattle rustlers who were preying on member's cattle.

Quanah prospered as a cattleman in Indian Territory, and represented the tribes well with the Washington politicians. He became a close friend of President Teddy Roosevelt, visiting in the White House and hunting wolves with him on the Comanche reservation.

Ned Armstrong and Jim's widow, Belle Cole, fought the state, railroads, cattle rustlers and sod busters to hang onto Ceebara---and young Cole and Jim Bold Eagle continued their friendship as they grew to manhood--but then, that's another story!

ABOUT THE AUTHOR

Gerald McCathern is a native of the Texas Panhandle, born in 1926, he has lived most of his life in the area around Amarillo.

After serving in the Aviation Engineers during WW II, he returned to Pampa, Texas, and worked in the oil fields for a short time before enrolling in Texas Tech under the G.I. Bill. It was there that he met and married his wife, Bonnie Traweek. He graduated from Tech with a degree in Petroleum Geology and worked on wild cat oil wells in the Permian Basin for a short time before moving to Hereford, Texas to begin a farming and ranching career.

Gerald has had an exciting life. In 1977 he became involved in the farmers' strike, known as the American Agriculture Movement. As the National Wagonmaster in that protest movement, he led over 5,000 tractors and 50,000 farmers across the nation to Washington, D.C. to carry their problems to Congress and the American people. As a spokesman of the movement, he appeared on Good Morning America and the Donahue Show, as well as on many radio talk shows, and met with the editorial board of the Washington Post. In 1981, President Reagan appointed him as Special Assistant to Secretary of Agriculture John Block in Washington, D.C. where he was instrumental in designing and implementing the cheese and surplus foods give-away program as well as many other constructive programs.

The tractor, which Gerald drove from Texas to Washington, D.C. the winter of 1979, is now enshrined in the Smithsonian Museum.

Gerald and Bonnie have three children and eight grandchildren.